Robert J. Ackerman, Ph.D.
and Dee Graham

Too Old to Cry

Abused Teens in Today's America

 Human Services Institute
Bradenton, Florida

TAB **TAB BOOKS**
Blue Ridge Summit, PA

362.76
A182t

Library of Congress Cataloging-in-Publication Data

ISBN 0-8306-3407-X (pbk.)

TAB BOOKS offers software for sale. For information and a catalog, please contact TAB Software Department, Blue Ridge Summit, PA 17294-0850.

Questions regarding the content of this book should be addressed to:

　　Human Services Institute, Inc.
　　P.O. Box 14610
　　Bradenton, FL 34280

Development Editor: Lee Marvin Joiner, Ph.D.
Copy Editor: Pat Hammond
Cover Design: Lori E. Schlosser

Dedication

To the Teenager within each of us:

May the process of this book
open doors,
cleanse the spirit
And help us to create
a safe Today.

Contents

Acknowledgments

The vision, patience and persistence of many individuals go into the writing and production of a book. Recognizing this, we wish to begin by thanking all those who contributed to the facts, stories, experiences, theories, and promises shared in this text. Sometimes it takes as much bravery to tell one's story as it does to become a survivor.

We also appreciate the wordsmiths and professionals who guided this book from concept to the concrete. We thank Lee Joiner for his editorial leadership and personal interest in seeing this project through and in helping all of us learn about ourselves. We thank Pat Hammond for the kind of critique that gives a manuscript strength and Marriette Petitpas for her dedication to detail and quiet encouragement.

Of course, we thank the staffs of Human Services Institute and TAB BOOKS, A Division of McGraw-Hill, Inc., for their willingness to support and believe in this book. It is their professional commitment that brings these words to public light.

Those who offer the most constant dedication to our efforts are our families, friends and intentional communities. They have seen the process of this book through personal crisis and intellectual activity. To those who have loved us and believed in us despite daily pressures, we offer a thank you that comes from our hearts.

1

Hitting Home
Trapped Teens in Abusive Families

What's so special about adolescent abuse? Child abuse has been so studied it sometimes seems like yesterday's news. What makes teenagers any different?

The answer comes as easily as the question. We expect teenagers to act more like adults, to be able to defend themselves and have enough sense to do so. But they don't.

Spouse abuse shelters are filled with teenage mothers who moved from violent, incestuous childhoods to being battered as adults. Juvenile shelters house delinquents who learned destructive behavior in abusive families, but take their own anger out in the only place they can—our communities. Little boys who had the "sense beat into them" brutalize our sisters and daughters, stepping on "weaker" women and children literally through rape and violence or figuratively by exerting dominating power in the workplace, the community and their own families. Women, also, are not immune to a violent reaction to an abusive upbringing and may perpetuate the cycle with their own offspring.

The world is reaching out to the children of these families. There are now some safe havens for victims of family violence. But when teenagers are involved, today's solution usually means juvenile detention or foster homes where none of the true needs of the youths are met.

Our society is in denial. It's easy to empathize with tiny, helpless little children whose parents hit or neglect them. But when the bruised or hurting victims look old enough to use self-defense, even though the batterer may be an adult on whose generosity their life depends, we see a different image.

Society Avoids Adolescents

Angry teenagers evoke less concern. For one thing, they appear physically at their peak. Their bodies seem fit and grown. Their anger scares us; their physical power gives them an aura of great strength. We fail to see the child within. We forget that these young people, while striving for independence, are relatively limited in what they can do for themselves in society. They need their families or another support system to survive. They are still learning what life's about; still discovering who they are.

It is precisely because teenagers are at that point in their lives when they are charting their adulthood that the problems of adolescent abuse and neglect are so important.

It is a time when they can reject the negative values of their dysfunctional families in favor of positive, humanistic ones. It is a time when they will learn about acceptance and rejection; a time when they will define success and determine their place in the world.

In a few years, they will be the adults and the rest of us will be the elderly. We will, in a sense, be in their charge. If we don't give them a strong sense of a positive self, if we don't speak to their pain and give them the tools to heal from an abusive or neglected childhood, then the anger that remains with them will continue to surface as they step into leadership roles.

How well adolescents do academically, a great indicator of how successful they will be in the world, is largely controlled by factors about which adolescents can do nothing. The truth is that nearly half the eighth grade students come from homes where one or more family issues affect their grades and test scores, according to a new study by the National Center for Education Statistics.

Forty-seven percent of the eighth graders studied live in a single-family home, have an annual family income of less than $15,000, stay home alone more than three hours a day, have parents without a high school diploma, have a brother or sister who is a high school dropout or have a limited English language proficiency. Over half, 53 percent, of the eighth graders have none of the six indicators. Twenty-five percent experience one, and 21 percent have two or more.

3

Even one of these risk factors put a child at risk for failure in school in a system that continues to function as though it were still serving children from traditional nuclear patriarchal families. Students with two or more of these six factors in their lives are twice as likely to place in the bottom quarter in school grades and reading and math test scores as those with none of the indicators. Only one in three eighth graders could show proficiency in analytical thinking skills in the reading and math tests given as part of the study. One in five cannot add, subtract, multiply and divide well enough for everyday needs.

The eighth graders studied spend four times as many hours watching television as doing their homework, and 27 percent of them are at home alone, without adult supervision, for at least two hours on school days.

Even if these adolescents are aware of the issues that complicate their ability to receive a good education, there seems to be nowhere to turn. According to the study, 54 percent of eighth graders never talk to a teacher about high school aspirations and 64 percent never discuss their future with a guidance counselor. Twenty-six percent never talk about the subject with their fathers either, although 31 percent live in households without fathers anyway.

Dysfunctional Families Produce Similar Problems

Troubled teens have similar stories. Bad attitudes, violent behavior, and anger turned inward result from a dysfunctional home that breeds unhappiness at best. That alone makes it difficult for a youth to adjust.

Consider the odds against Adam, whose first experience with something close to normalcy was in a group home for abused teens:

"My dad was a drug addict. My mother was an alcoholic and still is, and she was a drug addict," explains Adam. "I grew up in an abusive family—physical abuse and problems with suicide.

"My mom was thrown off the second story balcony by my dad. My dad always beat us. He beat my brothers.

"The only way I got to stay out until 1:00 A.M. was when I ran away. When I would come in my mom would always hit me. She would get my brother on the couch and whip his bare rear end with this wooden paddle.

"My dad was the same way. He would punch us. I could remember the times when he would punch me and almost knock me out from hitting my head against the furniture.

"My mom would throw things at me—knives. Every time she would go out I would throw a fit because she would go out and drink. I would say, 'I'm not staying home.' She would give me money to stay home. When she would go out, I would go out anyway. I would be there alone, me and my brother, until like 3:00 or 4:00 A.M.

"When she came home she would start to argue with us, swearing at and hitting us. If we were in bed, she would come and drag us out of bed and beat us up."

5

TOO OLD TO CRY

Whether the problems are as severe as Adam's or as clandestine as name-calling or absentee parenting, they all have serious impact on the lives of the youngsters who live through them.

Child Abuse is Part of World History

Child maltreatment is not a new phenomenon in society. It has existed over time and in every culture. No matter how it is defined, it means harm, as defined by the culture, to the child.

In ancient China, for example, little girls' feet were bound tightly and not allowed to grow, forcing them to stay close to home and obedient. If the family was poor enough, the young women were sold as concubines. These practices, which we see as extreme sexism and child abuse, were not only condoned, but also respected as a part of the culture.

The pain was no less for those little girls than it would be for children today.

In Charles Dicken's *Oliver Twist*, a young orphan boy is severely punished for asking for more food. As his rough life continues, he learns that being beaten with a rod and even murder may follow those who disobey the more powerful in their lives. This fictional tale alludes to the very real abuse of disenfranchised youth in Britain in the 1800s.

Our country has a history just as severe. Slave children were separated from their parents at the will of the plantation owner, instilling a sense of insecurity that surely harmed the parent-child relationship from day one.

Those children who survived intact in the slave family were expected to be docile and obedient. The slave owner's punishment for anything less could be swift, harsh, and violent, including severe beatings, loss of limbs, or even violent death. Under this system, Afro-American parents had to train their children to be compliant if they were to survive. They used a less severe, but still harsh, form of discipline.

Unrealistic expectations were also enforced. For example, during a slave escape even very young children could not be allowed to cry or walk slowly when tired. Any commotion from a youngster could endanger the lives of all, so the littlest ones had to learn to be silent and walk fast.

White families, too, endorsed violent discipline. Frontier schools made common use of the paddle and the dunce cap. Families of the 1800s often spanked their children at least once a week just for "good measure."

Society is Redefining What's Acceptable

Today, society is beginning to recognize that violence leads to violence; that abuse is not discipline. But definitions vary, and parenting techniques that have been passed down from generation to generation take concentrated effort to change.

What one individual views as discipline, another may consider abuse. A fine line divides the two. The definition of abuse or neglect reflects legal, ethical, moral, religious, political, and cultural dimensions. Some consider abuse to be a cultural problem, defined within a culture by its norms and values. One culture may consider violent methods of discipline acceptable, while another considers the same behaviors abuse.

Native Americans in Alaska, for instance, don't feel white people deserve children because they are so cruel as to strike them. They strongly disapprove of parents who get angry or yell at youngsters while cursing, slapping or hitting. Yet, although children are rarely punished in the Eskimo culture, the most common form of discipline there calls for plunging a crying infant into icy water.

This act would be considered child abuse by most U.S. social service agencies: the same ones who might hesitate to act against parents using a belt on their youngsters.

By today's standards, the three major elements to consider when distinguishing discipline from abuse are degree, duration, and intent of the punishment. A child who is slapped once, and no more, for breaking a dish may not be considered abused. However, a child who is smacked every day for not setting a table properly may be considered abused, especially if the child is injured by this discipline.

Many such judgment calls are left to social caseworkers or judges. Their ability to determine abuse stems from the

U.S. *Child Abuse Prevention Act of 1974*, which defines child abuse and neglect as:

> *... physical or mental injury, sexual abuse, negligent treatment or maltreatment of a child under the age of 18 by a person who is responsible for the child's welfare under circumstances that indicate that the child's health or welfare is harmed or threatened.*

The precise number of incidents of child abuse and neglect each year in the United States is unknown. Since the victims of these crimes are usually unaware of their rights or that what is happening to them is either abnormal or illegal, reports of abuse or neglect must number far fewer than the actual occurrence. Authorities estimate that more than one million children experience abuse or neglect each year. Some believe that from one to one and a half percent of youngsters in this country are abused. That amounts to ten to fifteen children per thousand people each year.

Sadly, the number of reported incidents of abuse and neglect is largest for infants. Adolescents are second, accounting for as many as 30 percent of reported cases.

The cases that make headlines are frequently those involving babies or small children. These little ones are unable to protect themselves, so they are perceived as extremely vulnerable to becoming victims. They are defenseless and demanding, requiring much of the parents' time and energy. They are nearly totally dependent on parents to meet their physical and emotional needs.

TOO OLD TO CRY

Teenage Victims Get Overlooked

In contrast, adolescents are less easily seen as victims because of their size and their capability for self-defense or flight. However, they are still likely victims, especially if the abuse began when they were young children. Patterns that begin that early are seldom easily broken. Children who come to expect to be hurt, who see pain and maltreatment as a normal part of life, may not realize their plight. In fact, they may become so accustomed to abuse that they feel something is wrong if they aren't being mistreated.

Teenagers are likely victims of abuse because of their emotional dependence on their parents, making them submissive to the abuse. The situation may be made worse when one of the parents allows himself or herself to be abused, teaching the children that it is normal to tolerate beatings or worse among adults.

Adolescents are also less likely to tell the truth about their abuse because they are aware of the social stigma. One sixteen-year-old recalls:

"My dad, he would always come home and beat up my mom. My mom would always, after he was done with her, take it out on me and my brothers and sisters because she wouldn't have nothing else to do. I guess her dad was the same way, the way my dad was, because when she was little it was the same type of situation.

"It happened all the time. Going through school I would always hide it . . . except for talking about how my dad got

10

into a fight with the cops last night. My dad is kind of crazy, but me and my dad always got along.

"My dad, my brothers and sisters, they never got along. My dad broke crutches over one brother and he beat up a lot of times my other brother. My oldest brother, he beat him up. My sisters, he would always beat them up.

"My mom would take it out on me what my dad did to her. She says one time that my dad, that he wishes we were never even born and that he wished we would all die. I remember my mom many times would tell me that she wished I was never born.

"Me and my mom always got into fights. Me and my dad always got along together great. I grew up and was with my dad. I was in the bars every day."

Many Factors Trigger Abuse

While the emotional attachment to parents is a major enabler of adolescent abuse, there are other triggers. Family stress, internal and external, can cause otherwise calm parents to revert to abusive or neglectful behavior. Developmental issues affecting both adolescents and parents or attempts at resolving family conflicts can blow up into violence.

Abuse is a complex phenomenon embedded within family systems. To understand the maltreatment of adolescents, one must know what is going on within both abusive and healthy families.

11

Not all abuse is physical. Name calling, unreasonable expectations and rules, inconsistent discipline, and general discouragement of the youngsters' interests are examples of mental or emotional abuse. Young people who have all their material comforts met may still suffer from neglect, needing from their parents what their parents don't know how to give.

Adolescents reared in abusive, neglectful, or simply dysfunctional homes haven't a clue about what a healthy family is like. They won't get it from history, friends, or textbooks. They won't learn how to enjoy life from religious doctrine or from hard discipline. What they need is prevention, intervention, and education. They need someone to care.

Sometimes the youths themselves can be reached and taught what a functional family is like. Sometimes they can even understand what must be done to change their own lives.

One teenager relates:

"I was reading a book. It says that it is not your fault. It's not because of you that your parents are alcoholics. You can't cure their disease. You definitely shouldn't try to control their alcohol abuse because all it does is make you feel afraid, on a guilt trip to come down on you because you are trying to control it.

"It is their fault because they are the ones that are drinking. If your parents say that 'If you wouldn't do this, maybe I would stop drinking' or 'Just stop hanging around with this friend or that friend and maybe I would stop drinking,' it really is not like that. No matter what you do or how you are, it is really up to your parents to stop.

"I would say that if you can't talk to your parents about it, then talk to a school teacher. Tell them the situation, then ask them what help options there are for yourself. A school teacher might know a little bit and point you to someone else to know a little bit more and get some help that way. Don't turn to drugs over it.

"The best thing to say is just to get out if you are having problems. Just get out of the house. There is always somewhere that you can get help. Hotlines. Toll free numbers. Get help.

"Myself, I learned the fact that parents aren't perfect. They make mistakes too. When you are old enough to make your own decisions, the choice is yours. Do what you want to do.

"If you want to follow in your parents' footsteps, then the choice is yours. The recovery program really does work if you want to work it. For myself, I had a lot of time clean and I ended up listening to my father and relapsing. I can't project it on my father though. Don't let your parents lead you in the wrong direction."

Most Adolescents Need Encouragement

That kind of independence is more than most teenagers can fathom. Few adolescents whose parents are actively

13

practicing abuse, neglect, and addictive behavior will actually be exposed by those parents to any recovery process. Even fewer youths will find their own way to Alateen or other self-help groups that may give them a way to see beyond their home life.

That's why there is such a need for adults to understand the problems abused and neglected teens face. That's why there's so much that needs to be done.

Of course, the other family members in these abusive or neglectful homes can't be ignored, or the problems will continue into the next generation. Parents who are willing to learn how to be proactive rather than reactive family leaders by participating in training classes, counseling, and support groups may set the best example for their offspring.

Adolescents are testing all things in life as they are becoming individuals. Sometimes the youths adopt abrasive tactics and their parents aren't sympathetic to their choices. Other times parents aren't aware of what their teenagers are doing because at these ages youths are doing all they can to fend off authority.

Like their parents, teenagers hear daily about the failure of the conventional family. Divorce rates continue to discourage belief in continuity. Yet, society has reached a point where single people are financially poorer than those who are married, especially women and mothers. Working single women trying to support the family as well as provide the nurturing often don't have the time they need to devote to adequate parenting.

In the U.S. today we must work much harder to reach the standard of living we enjoyed in the 1930s, 1940s, and 1950s. Today's parents may never have both the spacious home and the leisure time of previous generations. Also, the composition of today's families does not resemble yesterday's nuclear, patriarchal family. Yet society does not speak to the change. Religious institutions refuse to acknowledge acceptable alternatives and shame those who cannot or choose not to follow tradition. The business community continues to fight offering financial assistance for social issues ranging from quality day-care and health care to productive use of the elderly.

Everyone laments the problems. Some complain, yet offer no assistance or cooperation. Some blame the victims and move on. And while the issues continue to be ignored by those with the power to do something about them, our youths suffer the consequences.

In the U.S. today there is a growing concern for children. We are willing to help "innocent" youngsters, but there is total insensitivity for adults. In spite of recent efforts to help the homeless, when these disadvantaged children grow up into poverty as adults, the system turns a deaf ear.

Teenagers Are Stuck in the Middle

Adolescents are caught between the empathy our nation has for children and the coldness we show for disadvantaged adults. In the eyes of society, poor teenage moms quickly move from being perceived as precious little charity cases to system-abusing welfare mothers.

Even young people who want to move out of their troubled situations find little real opportunity. Our society has extended the once unknown period of adolescence to a developmental no-man's land. Teenagers and trainees (most of whom are adolescents) can be legally discriminated against simply because of age. If they are not victims of sexism, racism, classism, homophobia, ableism (discrimination against the physically challenged), or other forms of discrimination, they face a young version of ageism. They simply can't make it in a healthy way on their own.

These problems no longer belong only to someone else's family, someone else's children. Everyone is affected by adolescent abuse, whether in their home today or in the world at large tomorrow. No community is protected. No neighborhood is isolated from the effects.

If we hope to change the situation, we must begin by understanding the problem. That's what this book is about.

We begin by understanding the home life and values of these young people. We see how their parents reached the point of treating their families with abuse or neglect in a society that looks on dependent children as liabilities. We explore the real life impact of physical and emotional abuse and neglect, examining the daily life of these troubled teens and feeling the powerlessness of their plight.

Once we see the problem, we take a serious look at the danger signs. We identify symptoms, but we take it one step further. We critically examine what's being done today and why it isn't meeting the vast needs. We begin to understand why these adolescents need the help of the entire community, not just a few social service agencies or isolated caseworkers. We see what's involved in prevention and intervention to protect these young people by making the kinds of changes that affect the root issue rather than simply having a temporary cosmetic effect.

Finally, we look to ourselves. We see where we fit into the existing system and how we can influence change. We consider what realistic options are open to us if we choose to get involved in individual cases. What current institutions can be used to make a bad situation better?

Envisioning a Solution

There is a way out. It isn't an easy way. It isn't a solution we can leave to school authorities, court systems, or law enforcement. It involves a total consciousness of social change, a clear, decisive step away from acceptance of the discriminatory patriarchal social order toward an active belief in the basic worth and dignity of every human being.

If we turn our backs on our teenagers, we turn our backs on our futures. As we move toward a new century, we must move toward equality and justice for all—including adolescents.

2

Defining Values
What Makes This Family Different

In our homes, around the globe and particularly in the United States, the family is considered the basic unit of society. Although we live in a fast-paced world of changing times and trends, most people still seek and base their values on the existence of this mythical "perfect" family.

There are those who see the traditional patriarchal family of the 1950s—in the style of "Father Knows Best" —as sacred. The reality is that in the 1990s the nuclear family is fast disappearing. At the same time, more people are actively redefining the meaning of family in their lives. Refusing the limitations of yesteryear, they are leading a trend toward reevaluating our families of origin and the nuclear family's role in our greater society.

Today's families encompass many life choices and situations. The households in which children are growing up may include any combination of adults and children.

Youngsters may live with their married, biological birth parents; their parents and grandparents; a single parent; a parent, stepparent and step-siblings in a blended family; unrelated parents who choose to share a home; unmarried parents; lesbian or gay parents; foster parents with other children; or adults and children in collective living situations. There are a myriad of lifestyles and choices, but what families have in common is that they have greater influence than anything else in the children's lives.

Homes are places for nurturing and socialization, places to find security and protection. Our culture teaches us to expect support, love, and encouragement within our families. It is supposedly within this "safe haven" of our family that we learn to survive together.

It is possible for this to be a tremendously supportive system. Healthy adults and children can help each other to grow and feel strong. They can provide a home base where the members of the household can be themselves without fear, where they can turn in times of trouble, and where they can obtain a push when they need it.

Unfortunately, this isn't always the case. Relationships within families intensify. The goals of the family unit compete with individuals' needs and wants. This becomes particularly clear during a child's teenage years, when the family's need for bonding and home-based activities conflicts with the adolescent's need to define him- or herself, to explore relationships with peers, and to learn about the person he or she is becoming during the onset of puberty.

In the healthy family, young people have many opportunities to explore who they are and what life is about, but within safe boundaries set by benevolent parents. They are encouraged to make choices and decisions about themselves within a range of reasonable limitations. Through this process, children grow into maturity with security, self-esteem, and a belief in themselves. They learn about survival in terms of cooperation, support and protection.

It is a rare adolescent who has had this ideal sort of encouragement and guidance in childhood. Even educated, well-meaning parents have their own problems and their own priorities. Things happen that no one can control. Even the most positive period for any family is affected by four major factors: change, balance, communication, and mutual influence.

Taking the Challenge to Change

Change may be the only constant in the family situation. The entrance of children into an adult relationship or into the life of a single parent means major upheaval at best. No one can adequately prepare for the enormous job of parenting. Formerly self-centered adults must learn to balance their needs against those of an innocent yet demanding baby. Amid frequently unexpected new responsibilities, they must remember to take care of themselves and each other, as well as the newcomer. This alone creates a major challenge.

Besides the new responsibilities and the interruption of routines and sleeping patterns, adding an infant frequently

21

leads to greater division of labor. If the parents focus on these hardships, they are likely to find themselves deep in disagreement, conflict, depression and anger. If the parents' attitude is one of joy, however, the new stresses seem less overwhelming. Whichever attitude prevails strongly affects the resulting marital situation and the parent-infant relationships.

One study of newborns shows that the main distinction between secure and insecure infants stems not from the parents' upbringing or philosophy, but from the infant's own temperament. This was particularly true in the child's first three to nine months of life. After the babies were a year old, insecure children became even more unpredictable and unadaptable. The opposite was true of infants who were secure in their relationships with their mothers. For the family seeking to adjust to change, this suggests that the strength of child-parent bonding depends on both the parents' personalities and the child's temperament.

As they mature, families continue to change. Each member ages over time. Children and adults alike adopt new attitudes, beliefs, and emotional makeups as they grow. Often feelings and personalities change because of environmental factors—transitions in surroundings over which no one has control. This could be a major disaster such as a flood or earthquake. It could be as simple as new, undesirable neighbors or as great as a complete developmental transition such as when a contractor builds a high-rise next door.

Neighborhoods are surprisingly important. Mothers who view their neighborhoods somewhat negatively are the same ones who show insecure bonding with their infants. While this indicates only the women's perceptions of their neighborhoods, it clearly points to the impact of the social environment.

Situational factors also affect each family's development. An elderly grandparent may be added to a financially strapped household. An adult or adolescent may develop a chemical addiction. A parent with an unruly temper may cause violence to disrupt any growth process. On the other hand, an adult may earn a college degree and get a job that moves the family from a working-class to a middle-class lifestyle. Not all changes are bad, but all changes affect the family dynamics.

The Dance of Balancing

Throughout these changes, families try to maintain a sense of *balance*. This is the second factor that affects families. It's a continuous process, of course, since change is always taking place. With varying success and choreography, each member plays a role in the family's balancing process.

Keeping the balance is automatic and involves many conditions as well as personalities. It is this balancing act that happens when a baby enters an adult relationship, but the attempt for equilibrium continues and involves all family members. For example, the birth of twins into a family that includes older children puts those siblings into the role of helpers. With so much work and limited hands, the first-born naturally steps into responsibility—albeit too soon for his or her own personal development. In truth, no one may have asked this youngster to assume a parenting role, but the void had to be filled. Since they didn't verbalize the need, the adults may even be so busy they fail to recognize what has happened or to acknowledge the child's responsibility.

The dance of balancing is an unacknowledged phenomenon that uses coping methods either healthy or unhealthy, productive or addictive. When negative adjustment occurs, children compensate for addictive parents. Wives cover for alcoholic or abusive husbands. Husbands adjust to an unhappy marriage by workaholism.

A more healthy response might be a family council during which every person's feelings are considered, followed by an agreed-upon plan of action. But even still the balancing continues.

To attain and maintain balance, family members must discuss their feelings and ideas about the change that is occurring. This communication can take place verbally or nonverbally, but it must occur.

Any form of communication is good if it successfully lets the other family members know each person's feelings. But these messages are often misunderstood, leading to conflict. This is especially true if the individuals attempt to protect themselves by manipulation and power plays geared to make others respond in expected patterns. Like a well-greased mousetrap, pushing the right emotional buttons causes other levers to move and other patterns to proceed. In the final analysis, everyone gets caught.

Mutual influence is unavoidable. Within a family, each member's attitudes, beliefs, ideas, and behaviors affect the other members. Differences in attitudes and beliefs can cause conflict and strife as individuals take opposing sides. It is the kind of situation feared by those who refuse to discuss politics or religion.

These four factors are neither positive nor negative. They simply show the ways families interact. In functional, nonabusing families, change, balance, communication, and mutual influence are used to adjust to everyday situations and crises. The members learn to resolve conflicts peacefully and respectfully. They develop healthy, productive mechanisms for coping with change. Together they learn to meet each other's needs—individually and as a group.

Members of nonabusing families support one another and depend on each other. They know how to negotiate and compromise, and how to give and take to meet each other's needs. With respect for each person's dignity, they find creative, nonviolent ways to handle the stresses they face, to meet needs, and to handle change.

Healthy families aren't afraid of the system, although they may not buy into the entire package. They take the responsibility to make themselves aware of community resources that provide natural support systems. This may be as simple as making sure a school-age child has the opportunity to play Little League Baseball, or as direct as networking with the public school to provide counseling for a confused adolescent. But they make sure each family member's needs are met and they use the system to their advantage regardless of financial status.

In contrast, members of abusive families fail to support each other positively. It has little to do with desire or good intentions. A parent may truly love a child but be so caught up in his or her own dysfunctional behavior that the child's needs are overlooked or misinterpreted.

Again, communication is vital. Dysfunctional families are unable to get the message across. Members don't know each others' desires or needs even when they think they do. Father can't know best, because father didn't stop to listen to the problem. A teenager's emotional crisis may be overlooked because her bravado keeps her from showing her true pain. Yet parents wonder why whatever they do doesn't fix the situation.

Lack of support and poor communication frequently result in family members who are so loosely bonded that they function independently of each other. They may see each other only in passing, or they may be in the same room frequently yet never speak about matters of importance.

Factors That Make the Difference

The difference between functional and dysfunctional interaction stems from the ways families deal with several conditions. Often these conditions cause a breakdown of the working family system. These stressful factors are:

1. Environmental chance factors can so seriously alter a family situation that the functioning system no longer works. For example, if a hurricane levels the

family home, suddenly the individuals are forced to cope with cramped temporary living spaces, the inability to control their day-to-day life, and financial stress.

2. Environmental stress factors can critically affect the family's ability to cope with change. Pressures of the day can force a crisis that totally destroys the group balance. Some examples are unemployment, poverty, insufficient education or a new baby.

Consider what happens when a family is forced to relocate to a new community where no one has outside friends or support systems. Pressure increases on the family unit as everyone meets new challenges in daily life, whether at new jobs, new schools, or in new forms of recreation. Tension builds and individuals turn to ineffective coping strategies.

Simply living as a minority in a dominant culture other than the family's native culture gives environmental stress factors major impact. If there is a relatively small degree of "fit" between the cultural patterns of the group and the host culture, the family experiences more difficulty. The extent to which ethnicity affects individuals' behavior and attitudes depends on the "ethnic density"—the size of the supportive community sharing cultural or moral values as a minority.

How far this pressure goes and whether it leads to maltreatment within families depends on the social resources available. Again, cultures that place a high value on caring for children deflect stress away from youngsters and their care-givers.

Rates of particular kinds of maltreatment also are related to the immediate culture's beliefs about special categories of children such as the physically challenged or illegitimate and beliefs about age capabilities and child development.

Finally, the degree of embeddedness of child rearing in kin and community networks is clearly reflected in the value placed upon those youngsters as individuals.

It is important to remember that, while the ethnicity of the family and its immediate community can largely shape its value structure and its attitudes toward children, in the United States many ethnic and cultural minorities are quick to assume the dominant social values. Some integrate quickly into the national culture, while others remain largely alien despite the pervasiveness of society.

3. When one or more family members suffer from deviance and pathology, group balance can be nearly impossible. The deviant individual lacks an ability to assume responsibility, and fails to function effectively socially, intellectually, or emotionally. The person can't carry his or her own share of the group load due to psychological problems; thus the burden falls to the rest. The impact of this situation greatly affects the overall health of the entire family.

4. Dysfunctional behavior by an individual family member, particularly a parent, can prove disastrous for the

children. An alcoholic parent frequently produces an alcoholic adult child, a behavior certainly influenced by the youngster's observations of the parent's coping choices. An abusive parent often brings up a child who also abuses his or her own children, particularly when no other mode of discipline was used at home.

Some addictions are considered positive in the eyes of society. Workaholics may be assumed to be self-sacrificing for the good of the family rather than seen as avoiding emotional intimacy. Exercise addicts may be thought of as healthy, although they may be using athletics to prove themselves strong and powerful.

There is a trap inherent in addictive behavior. Whether chemically or emotionally bound, many addicts find the roots of their coping choices in childhood experiences remembered as gratifying. That is one reason the addictive behavior feels so irrationally good to the dysfunctional person. The addiction reminds him or her of an earlier, safer feeling. The desire to recapture that security is a wish that becomes a self-perpetuating trap.

In addition, there is increasing evidence that genetic tendencies are the most important factors in food, alcohol, sex, and other addictions. This means that children and teenagers being raised in addictive households are by nature at high risk for repeating the cycles themselves in their adult lives. Science concludes that the genetic makeup of a person is the foundation upon which one builds coping skills and strategies.

Families don't have to appear abusive to the outsider to have problems with addiction or dysfunctional coping. Anytime stress becomes nearly unmanageable within a family structure, dysfunction is possible. Often, neglect or abuse will follow.

It is vitally important at these times that social isolation not occur. A lack of emotional support resources, inadequate coping abilities, or the absence of any external or community support system leads directly to a negative family atmosphere.

Ways Families Dysfunction

While these factors appear in all families, certain types of people face more challenge in these areas than others. The ways families dysfunction can be grouped into six categories:

1. Extreme isolation

   These families have little support from their members, friends, relatives, neighbors, or religious groups. They keep to themselves with few exceptions.

2. Extreme social involvement

   Rather than isolation, these families become so involved with outside activities that the internal family structure becomes fragmented. External integration takes place when family members have little time for one another. Instead, they find support among people outside the family group.

3. Lack of bonding

Although some family members may develop strong ties, others are left out. An example of this is when a strong emotional link develops between a mother and daughter, but the father is excluded from their activities together. He is hurt and has no opportunity to form bonds with his child. Eventually he and other excluded family members usually begin to have trouble handling stress and change. Another danger here occurs when one parent uses the child as a weapon against the other.

4. Unintended family group

In today's me-first culture, parents often ignore their youngster's rights and even needs. The adults put themselves first, meeting their own needs before those of their children. This situation reaches a serious level when the parents begin to feel they are the only people in the family. An inaccurate perception of children as incomplete human beings develops, causing a lack of respect for the younger individuals.

5. Immaturity of family

Family members may repeatedly fail to meet each other's needs, either emotionally or physically. The family's security is threatened when parents and children fail to nurture one another. The entire family group thus fails to mature and functions only ineffectively.

6. Chemical addiction

Dysfunctional families frequently result from drug or alcohol abuse. This is especially dangerous or abusive when the parents or children become involved in illegal activities.

While these indicators can be observed in any family of any background, clearly a consideration of socioeconomic class also must be made.

There are other common sense influences that determine a family's potential for dysfunction and its practical ability to overcome external influences and move toward healthy interactions. The amount of quality time parents have to spend with their children is largely influenced by working requirements, educational attainment, and financial status. A working mother trained only for evening waitress work has little chance to bond with and influence her children the way a stay-at-home physician's wife can.

Money Eases the Problem

Money also controls parents' abilities to enjoy personal recreation during child-free time, to afford comfortable medical care, to serve nutritious meals, and to provide many of the comforts of life that make the difference in any person's ability to cope with stress.

Many coping mechanisms are more accessible for families with adequate financial resources. Alcohol and drug treatment centers cost significant amounts of money, even when the family has medical coverage. Community resources, while sometimes available to the lowest economic strata, are hardest for working class families to access. Wealthier families may be able to afford the finest counseling centers, parenting classes, and educational environments. These are the resources that can make the difference for borderline dysfunctional families.

All families face difficulties, but without adequate finances the solution to problems is much farther from reach. Individuals who have no means of making a living or for getting help find themselves in a self-perpetuating cycle. They need education. They need counseling or advice. They need release from daily stress, but they can't stop working to stay home. If they receive government aid, they may be unable to make enough money to support their family, yet they may be held back from contributing what little they can because that income would disqualify them.

Summary

No family is typical today. Times are changing and so is the definition of a family. However, regardless of the composition of the family unit, certain stress factors affect how we relate together. We must deal effectively with these stressors if we are to keep the family healthy. Of course, the burden will be greater on those who are economically disadvantaged. Only by education and awareness of the problems can we begin to reach toward full social change.

3

Misplaced Violence
Parents Who Abuse

It's the rare parent who has never ever spanked a child. It isn't that we haven't tried other things first. It isn't that we expect the spanking to work better than any other form of discipline. It's simply that we're hurried, angry, or tired and just don't know what else to do. It's usually the last resort in a frustrating struggle with an ornery child.

While a single swat on the bottom with a bare palm may not fall into the realm of legal child abuse, its results are usually ineffective. This is almost always true of physical punishment. Except for shock value, spanking just doesn't work. We may have learned this fact in parenting courses, through educational training, or from experience, but that doesn't stop us from reacting to a difficult situation with our first impulse.

We aren't alone. That's why abuse can happen even in a perfectly functional family. A family is made up of individuals. Parents are people first—adults or young people with their own wants, needs and behavior patterns. Only when we consider who these parents are do we begin to see the whole picture. We need to know their characteristics and understand their personalities before we can understand why they abuse.

Who Are the Abusers?

What differentiates the abusive parent from one who only occasionally loses his or her temper and spanks a child? The distinction is fine. Somewhere, somehow that nonabusive parent learned self-control. That parent knows when to stop.

Abusive parents don't know how to control their reactions. They don't sense the difference between a single spanking and a battering, between an instant response and a tirade. They lose control of themselves and of their child. Panic ensues. They react with violence.

Losing control isn't pleasant. Angela felt she was prepared for motherhood when she decided to become a single parent. She planned the baby's nursery, signed up for the right preschools, and enrolled in parenting classes. She sincerely wanted the best for her child and she felt sure she could give her daughter the best.

Then, the child began to grow up. Heather was a strong-willed little individual, demanding attention and always getting her way. By the time the little girl reached age four, she was running Angela's life.

Frustrated, strung out, and physically exhausted, Angela stopped having the mental strength to think faster than her daughter. Listening to well-meaning friends, she discovered that when she threatened to spank Heather with a wooden spoon she felt renewed power. She believed that was her job as a parent—to control her child's behavior. Reluctantly, she began to rely more and more on physical discipline.

Anger mounted. Money problems, feelings of loneliness and desperation weighed heavily on Angela. As a single mother, she had nowhere else to turn for help or support. Only her little girl was there, and the relationship seemed more and more to be draining rather than rewarding.

Angela never would have called herself abusive. She just had a problem child, she believed. She just needed help—another adult to share the responsibility. Still, there was no one. She let no one know the depth of her desperation.

Angela's built-up anger took control of her the night Heather broke her late grandmother's antique vase. For the young mother there was no holding back. Angela was barely aware of her actions as she grabbed the child's arm, held her down on the bed and hit her repeatedly with the spoon.

The next day, even Angela was shocked by the bruises on the little girl's legs. She dressed her daughter in long pants and sent her to school, vowing never to lose control again.

But she did. Angela was past the point of stopping, past the point of self-control.

Parents like Angela have lost the ability to keep their life in perspective. There is no one point at which people lose control. Each of us has a different breaking point at which we finally give in to the pressure. Pent up emotions have no place else to go and eventually burst out when we have little control over them. If we are parents, our children are likely to suffer.

Healthy people recognize their feelings and know safe ways of expressing anger or frustration. Functional parents lead their children rather than demand power over them. They see their little ones as individuals rather than extensions of themselves that must be controlled.

Abusive Parents Lack Perspective

Abusive parents generally lack this perspective. They seldom mean to seriously harm their youngster. They may love their offspring as much as healthy, effective parents. However, they haven't learned certain basic lessons about life.

Parents who resort to physical abuse don't know how to get their own needs met. Like Angela, these parents become frustrated and desperate when they have no appropriate way to take care of themselves. Coping behaviors that may have worked for them as child-free adults or when they themselves were children are no longer possible. A night out at the bars can't be the answer to a bad day at work when there are children to be fed, bathed, and put to bed. Hiding under the covers with ice cream and a romance novel doesn't get the children's homework done or take care of the laundry.

Parents who aren't taking care of themselves lack the maturity to care for their children. It has nothing to do with intent, because they may care very much about their offspring. They just don't have the resources to see what they're doing to themselves and their families.

Abusive Parents Neglect Themselves

Abusive parents fail to realize they are responsible only for their own actions. It's easier to worry about others than to take responsibility for our own difficulties. Without examining ourselves, we point out to others what they fail to see about themselves. We give ourselves the job of making our family or friends happy, ignoring our own needs, or expecting someone else to take care of us. We gain self-esteem by helping others, but we put ourselves in personal jeopardy when we are forever taking care of others but neglecting ourselves.

This is what happens with abusive parents. They don't realize what their own needs are or that those needs aren't being met. In fact, it is likely these adults were never adequately taken care of by their own parents. If they grew up in a dysfunctional family themselves, they may have had to learn to take on the role of caretaker for their parents or siblings. They may have felt pressure to "fix" their family of origin rather than learning to care for themselves. If they felt they were to blame for other family members' dysfunctional behavior, they probably never developed enough self-esteem to nurture themselves.

When these people have children, their sense of responsibility for others becomes greater. They spend even less time taking care of themselves. Instead, their children's behavior becomes paramount. This is the adults' chance to prove themselves worthy by producing children of whom they can feel proud. How these parents judge themselves depends on what others think about the children or the family. The youngsters are expected to accept the parents' values rather than develop independence. Everything the children do is seen as vital, yet the parents continue to ignore their own needs.

These parents clearly have a confused sense of responsibility. They run from their feelings and keep busy with other people's problems—usually their children's business. They neglect or abuse themselves by compulsive behaviors such as alcoholism or workaholism. At the same time, they overcompensate by trying to maintain absolute control over their children. They make inappropriate decisions about family issues, believing they are doing what's best for their children. They discourage their youngsters' personal growth by making decisions for them. They spend hard-earned money on expensive toys or impressive clothing, which their children may not want, yet they neglect medical bills. They ignore their own personal emotional necessities, especially the adult time they need for self-preservation.

Feelings and Actions Get Confused

The difference between feelings and actions frequently confuse abusive parents. Unless individuals are taught that their feelings have value, they may never allow themselves to acknowledge fully their hurts or their happiness. Sadness or pain, held over perhaps from the parents' own childhoods, settle into them. As with Angela's broken vase, these feelings emerge years later as anger or rage far stronger than that merited by a single incident. Even happiness can cause unexpected behaviors if it isn't expressed in a healthy manner or trusted (*Something will break the spell so it might as well be me*).

When feelings are repressed or denied over time, they become very confusing. People who have held back their emotions will automatically respond to a difficult situation with a total loss of control. For example, a child's temper tantrum could trigger the parents to scream and hit. They don't have the inner calm that would allow them to find a more effective response such as calmly holding the youngster and speaking directly to the out-of-control child. Instead, the parents are also out of control. The adults don't connect their responses to their own past. They don't realize that their deep feelings of frustration can be dealt with without hitting or violence. They respond without feeling or thinking.

Failing to deal with their feelings leads adults to other problems. Making decisions can be an impossible task for abusive parents. If we're going to be effective parents, we have to think faster and clearer than our children. We need to respond to problems with a calm understanding and foresee the logical consequences of our actions. We need to distinguish between problems that are ours and problems that really belong to our children. We need to learn to make those decisions rapidly and rationally.

Abusive parents can't make those decisions. They don't have enough information. They already feel confused about themselves. They are seldom calm enough to judge a situation correctly or to see the source of the problem. They snap back at a youngster without understanding why. They respond with discipline that far outweighs the seriousness of the misbehavior.

Being unable to make decisions about their own lives gives abusive parents constant variables to deal with. They aren't in control of themselves or the course of their lives. They can't count on anything because nothing around them is stable. No choice is final. No action can be counted on. This gives them little chance to make effective decisions regarding their parenting or anything else in their lives.

Also, partly because they are trying too hard to be responsible for others, abusive parents get their self-esteem from the way their family members respond to them. What the children do is all-important because the parents have no inner source of personal affirmation. So much is at risk in their child's behavior that if a youngster breaks an expensive item out of frustration, because what he or she really needed was a trip to the dentist to fix a hurting tooth, parents react with violence. Insulted that the toy isn't appreciated, well-meaning parents lash out in anger. The problem and its cause are never connected. The parents feel worse because they were counting on their children to provide them with a positive self-image.

This predicament is especially exaggerated when parents have ignored their own care as well. They resent what they have given up "for" the children, though the children didn't ask the parents for self-denial. The adults may even feel the child "owes" them for this "sacrifice," worsening the problem.

Parents Sometimes Have to Wait

Another difficulty for parents who become abusive is learning how to delay gratification. Patience is not always a welcome virtue, yet this quality is a mainstay of effective parenting. Few children learn a lesson the first time. It is a rare child who responds immediately to even the best adult leadership. They always test the boundaries of any care-giver or any situation, because that's how youngsters learn.

Abusive parents can't wait out a child's testing period. They expect perfection and expect it immediately. This demand is especially magnified when the parents' self-esteem rests on the children's behavior. Any delay or infraction cited by the parents, even those caused by unrealistic expectations, translate to the children as personal failure. If the little ones' feelings of inadequacy are reinforced by punishment or abuse, a self-fulfilling prophecy may be set into motion. Even as adults, the children may never believe they can succeed in life. They expect more of themselves than is normal, but they hate themselves for not meeting the perfectionist standards they learned from their parents.

As adults, the inability to delay gratification carries over into the abusive parents' treatment of themselves. They act impulsively. They can't wait for what they want when they see it. They want it now and nothing will stand in their way.

They want instant gratification so badly because they deprive themselves of daily caretaking. Daily, they avoid dealing with their true feelings through addiction or escapism. This takes the form of an activity that keeps the adults too busy to be effective parents or an addiction that makes the parents inaccessible physically or emotionally. Being responsible for children means being available to them even when it would be more gratifying to be doing something else—sleeping, taking care of business or having a good time.

When abusive parents, particularly those with chemical addictions, are required to postpone what they want to do to care for children, they resent the demand. They don't want to take the time to deal with their children's problems. They want to settle the situation as quickly as possible. If they dominate or gain control through abuse, they may be able to quiet the child and move on to self gratification.

Impulse ridden adults are at great risk of becoming abusive parents. They respond without thought and show little self-control. When the impulse strikes, they act. They hurt. They don't stop to think, but the mark they leave on their children lasts much longer than the physical pain.

Parenting Means Long-Term Commitment

There is another way the inability to delay gratification or wait for results comes into play in parenting. Dysfunctional parents may not be looking at raising the child as a long-term effort. They may know that rearing a child takes about twenty years, but their eyes are only on the present. Abusive parents see one behavior or situation on a single day as much more important than it actually is. They forget the big picture.

Even healthy, active parents can lose their balanced perspective after a difficult day or when the stress level is high. It might occur in a grocery store when a child knocks a product off the shelf. To the casual observer, it may be shocking if the parents shows little reaction to the misbehavior. Shoppers see only the single incident. They don't realize the misbehavior is only one infraction in a full day of taxing child care. They aren't aware of the stress the family may be suffering. Upsetting a grocery display may be minor when seen in relationship to other things that have happened to the youngster in the previous twenty-four hours. Being able to put children's behavior in perspective is part of effective parenting.

All these skills contribute to the quality of an individual's life, particularly if that person is a parent. Adults who lack these abilities, however, feel out of control and helpless. They are unable to meet their own needs. As a result, they have no idea how to meet the needs of their children.

Healthy Families Find a Successful Formula

Personalities obviously play an integral role in the occurrence of abuse within a family situation, but there's more to the picture. Real life places a combination of personalities in a family setting. To that formula, society adds environmental and social factors that impact on the family unit and influence how parents act. Even healthy adults are likely to revert to less appropriate behaviors when dealing with overwhelming external stress.

A family that moves frequently, for example, lacks the ability to maintain routine or security in a home situation. The stress of moving, by itself, weakens everyone's coping abilities. Children act out their feelings of fear or discomfort in a new school or new neighborhood. New jobs bring new demands on the adults. Moving costs add to financial pressure. When this happens to overtaxed parents, abuse is a likely result.

Financial difficulty places a heavy burden on parents with a propensity toward violence. Without enough money to meet the children's and their own basic needs, they feel even less worthy. In a society that values status, these parents strike out where they can. The poorer the family, the less personal power and privilege the parents can have. When the only place they can feel in control is in their home, the children suffer.

Social isolation, provoked by frequent moving or financial inability to socialize, creates fertile ground for abuse. Having fewer friends and acquaintances makes it easier for signs of abuse to be covered up. The less the outside world knows, the more control the parents have. The less their children know about other people, the more likely it is they will follow their parents' ways and accept abuse or neglect as normal.

Parents who have unrealistic expectations of their children may use violence as a means to push them harder. Although children develop in identifiable stages, adults who are unaware of age-appropriate behavior can't understand what they can really expect of their children. If they feel responsible for making the youngsters meet their own unrealistic standards, they are tempted to turn to physical abuse for control.

Misplaced emotions also come into play when parents who feel powerless in the world take their anger or frustration out by physically battering their children. Again, their home may be the only place where these adults can show any power. They carry in anger from outside, where they have no acceptable outlet. They carry resentment, fear and other personal issues. The children face the brunt of these emotions, having no safe place to turn.

Children Can't Parent Their Parents

Without adequate adult support systems, parents turn to their children for nurturing or help with responsibilities. A child cannot be an adult's confidant. This is an unhealthy role reversal. Yet, isolated adults who are unable to cope with crises do turn to their children. They need support, encouragement or someone to listen. But they need adults, not youngsters. Even adolescents aren't ready to be their parents' confidants or best friends. It is another version of role reversal.

The parent's dependent relationship may give children a temporary burst of self-esteem. It is flattering to have adults turn to them, to have grown-ups value their opinions. But it is also deceiving. When adults turn to children, the youngsters believe they have the power to help. In reality, children are basically powerless. Not realizing this, they try to "fix" the parents' problems and feel utterly discouraged when they can't help at all. They may be totally confused about what to do and get angry with themselves for failing to do the impossible.

In some families the children are leaned on for even more than emotional backup. Expecting a child to financially support the family, take over the parenting of younger siblings or to run a household are forms of abuse. These parents may totally deny that they are shirking their duty. They themselves are overwhelmed with the tasks and responsibilities of raising a family. They don't want to believe they need their children to take care of them, yet they can't do it all themselves.

When this happens, children are forced to grow up without experiencing the growth process of childhood. They are denied essential development periods in life. They spend so much energy caretaking their parents or other family members that they, like their parents before them, never learn how to nurture themselves. They may even hate themselves for failing to make things change for the better.

Self-Hatred Breeds Hate

Low self-esteem clearly leads people to be abusive. Parents who hate themselves will find it hard to like anything or anyone in their lives, including their children. They have little basis for judging situations, little foundation for creating a positive family experience. At the same time, they feel more need to see their children excel and turn to abuse as a way to control their offspring.

Self-hatred, fear, and low self-esteem build walls. Without an ability to be empathic or to respect and understand the feelings of another, parents fall into abuse. They can't sense the pain their youngsters feel. They don't see the impact of their behavior or the hurt they cause their children.

A belief in punishment is integral to child abuse. Some parents think they are doing the right thing by physically hurting children who misbehave. They subscribe to dominance in their parenting style, believing they are correct in teaching children to fear authority figures through violence and force. They may even believe this will protect their children when they grow up. They are teaching their children the fears they themselves harbor.

Abusive parents don't have fun. They don't know how to find pleasure themselves. They may be uncomfortable when things are calm or pleasant, because they may never have felt comfortable inside themselves. When all their experience has been bleak and marred with struggle, few positive solutions seem reachable. They may turn to addictive behaviors——drinking, overeating, workaholism

—to hide from their own pain. Parents who are this unhappy rarely raise happy children.

A fear of spoiling the children also can cause parents to use physical violence. Because so many abusive parents learned their behavior and coping styles from their families of origin, they believe they must be strict parents. They may have a sincere desire to protect their children from an overindulgent life in a permissive family, but the parents overreact when their actions turn to abuse.

Destructive Patterns Can Be Identified

Naturally, not all these characteristics or behavior patterns exist in all abusive homes. Parents are as individual as anyone else. The families that dysfunction do so in many ways and with many variations. There is no typical example, only commonalities. The complexities and evolvement of destructive behaviors that result in abusive families are the subject of much study and analysis. What we do know is that they interplay with disastrous results.

There are many ways we can recognize these telltale abusive patterns within the families we encounter. Parental immaturity is revealed in relationships with children and others. Often these parents have the emotional and mental makeup of children, but try to live adult roles. They are what is known as "adult children." They have an egocentric world view and understand situations only as they affect themselves. These parents become so involved in meeting their own needs that they see their children's needs as irrelevant.

Look for a family lacking friends or community. These are clear candidates for a violent home life. Abusive parents not only isolate themselves physically, but separate themselves emotionally and verbally from other family members or friends. This also occurs in a couple where one spouse is abusive and the other remains more passive, perhaps even being the target of abuse as well.

Isolated, abusive families wait for others to approach them. They are unlikely to belong to social organizations or community groups. They view other people as enemies and therefore hesitate to make friends or let others into their lives.

This isolation can begin with the parents' low self-esteem. Parents who feel unworthy or unlikable believe anything they do is of little value. They don't circulate in the community because they fear or have experienced rejection. If they have little money, they may prefer to stay at home rather than appear poor in comparison to their neighbors or associates. They internalize these things, blaming themselves and feeling worse about themselves. This hinders their ability to make decisions and keeps them from taking proper leadership roles even within the family.

Teenage Parents Face Greater Risk

Becoming a mother or father requires only a biological function, so it isn't surprising that many people are inadequately prepared for parenting. This is especially true of teenagers who find themselves facing unplanned pregnancies. They are unprepared for parenthood, yet these young women are increasingly deciding to carry their pregnancies to term and keep the babies.

Still children themselves, adolescent parents have little idea of how healthy families live. Chances are they haven't experienced enough growing up to understand what childhood is really about. They may never have received positive parenting in their families of origin. Having little experience in the world, they may have no idea of the ways functional families work. Even those who grew up in nurturing home environments have little preparation for the responsibilities that accompany parenthood.

Teenage parents, many of whom are single mothers, commonly face a greater challenge than they can meet. With no idea of what's reasonable, these unprepared young parents have unrealistic expectations of their offspring. They don't know what babies or children require or what can be expected of them. When the children inevitably fail to meet their parents' expectations, the parents try to exert more control. They want to force their youngsters to "behave." They don't understand why their children don't meet their unrealistic standards.

When Children Don't Respond, They Push Harder

Abuse follows as these parents try even harder to make their children conform. Parents respond to what they perceive as resistance with physical or emotional overreaction.

Abuse occurs when parents interpret certain age-appropriate behaviors as "willful disobedience" or intentional behavior as when the child opposes the parents' commands. These people believe their children are defying orders; refusing to do as they're told to simply to rebel against their parents. The parents just don't understand that the children can't comply.

Parents lose control when they believe their children's "misbehavior" occurs because of "bad dispositions." They see their youngsters as "stubborn," "unloving" and "spoiled." They blame the children's personalities rather than seeing that as parents they are setting unreasonable standards.

Being unfamiliar with the ways healthy families work can create a potentially abusive situation. Without role models or personal experience in a functional household, adults can't be the leaders in their own homes. What parents then expect from their children adds to the pressure their offspring must face.

Children Carry Heavy Burdens

Some parents view their children as extensions of themselves. Young parents or adults with low self-esteem start with great hope for their little ones. They see in their babies a second chance to make something of themselves. They believe their children are responsible for fulfilling their own desires. They want the best for them, but they also place on their children the mantle of fulfilling the family dreams.

Children naturally accept these expectations. They don't know any better. They don't know what to expect of themselves. They want to please their parents so they try to do what's asked. Naturally, they cannot measure up to the roles set forth. They cannot fix their parents. They can't do the impossible. What happens is that these children, in turn, feel worthless.

Unless the family faces the situation realistically and attempts recovery from dysfunctional patterns, the chain reaction continues. The parents begin to feel like they themselves have failed a second time when their children disappoint them.

Perhaps because there must be some break in this stressful evolution, parents and children in abusive families spend little quality time together. They touch each other infrequently and rarely talk about their feelings. Hugging or praise occurs rarely.

Since children learn through conversation and body language, without touch or attention they are left with an unclear idea of what behavior is expected of them. Without feedback, they are less likely to comply with parental rules. Since they are unfamiliar with what they can expect of themselves, they can't communicate with their parents about their feelings or needs. The parents, who see only disobedience or misbehavior, take a more negative attitude toward their children.

Summary

When parents become abusive it is usually in response to many things that are dysfunctional within their lives. They may have been abused themselves, never developing self-esteem, and never learning appropriate ways of interacting with others. Their hurtful behavior may be a negative response to their immaturity and lack of understanding about children. Or they may be reacting to external influences—financial stress, educational or cultural disadvantages or life changes with which they cannot cope. The youngsters in these households face the brunt of their parents' powerlessness. In turn, the children may feel responsible for "fixing" the family's problems or taking care of their dysfunctional parents.

Only when these families no longer find themselves lost in misplaced expectations of themselves and those around them will they find their way from abuse and dysfunction to a healthy lifestyle.

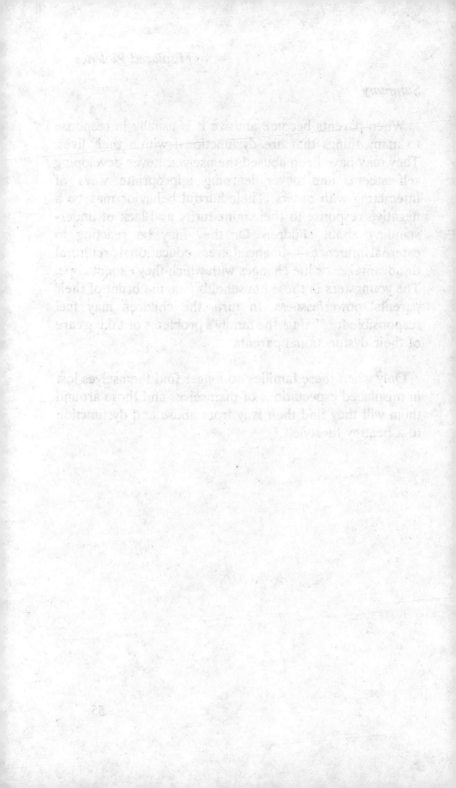

4

Sins of Omission
Parents Who Neglect

Doing nothing wrong can be the same thing as doing nothing right. You're still doing nothing.

This is true in the workplace, where no work means no pay. It's true in school, where no homework means no grade. And it's true in parenting, where lack of attention and love can be devastating.

Doing nothing is the error made by neglectful parents.

Children who come home from school every afternoon to a beating may have an unnatural perception of love and attention, but they *do* get noticed. However misdirected the attention, they're at least worth the bother of negative attention. They know that their presence—even if resented—has the power to make their family respond. It isn't healthy, but it's something.

Neglected children may never feel the ache of a bruised leg or the agony of incest, but they live with a deep pain that may never get expressed or acknowledged. They live daily with undeserved shame and a very real fear of abandonment, feelings for which they probably have no validation or outlet. There is no language that addresses the nonexistent, no hot line for loneliness.

Many of us were taught that if we ignore the things that bother us, they will go away. It's an idea that works much of the time. If we fail to feed the sea gulls on the beach, they eventually seek scraps elsewhere. If we hang up on telephone solicitors, the sales talk ends.

People who work with scientific behavior modification have a similar theory. Their studies have shown that if we want to stop or "extinguish" a behavior, such as a friend's annoying dinnertime phone calls, we need to fail to respond or "reinforce" that act. For example, if the bothersome ring is never answered when meals are being served, then the friend learns to call at other times or not at all. The unfortunate catch is that irregular or "intermittent" reinforcement encourages a behavior more than consistent or constant response. If we forget and answer the inconvenient call just once, we've encouraged the person to try again and again.

The same dynamics are at work in the family. No matter what the neglectful parent may wish, ignoring a child does not lessen the responsibility or erase the youngster. It may, however, affect the child's behavior and feelings.

Communicating the Silent Message

The silent message a neglectful parent communicates is far different from the angry lashing out of an abusive one. It is the message that "If I ignore you, you'll go away. I don't want you." The reason behind the parents' lack of attention doesn't matter to the child. Even teenagers are rarely mature enough to recognize that parents are humans with normal successes and failures. Youths don't understand that their parents' attitude toward them may have nothing to do with them, despite the fact that it affects them. To children, the parents they know are their world. Without caretakers, usually parents, a child cannot survive.

This direct dependency places children and adolescents in an awkward situation. The very people who may abuse or neglect them are the ones who make their survival possible. As dependents, they have great stake in keeping their parents satisfied with them and great risk if they alienate their only support network. This is true even if the network has holes in it.

Youths whose parents neglect them may easily conclude that the lack of attention or care is their own fault. They feel if they could just behave better, make better grades, or look a few pounds thinner, then their parents would notice. Then they would be good enough.

Children have a right to a certain amount of attention and physical provisions. In today's patriarchal system, based on the nuclear family structure, it is the parents' job to be caretakers. The parents are expected to provide for those whom they have created or for whom they have assumed legal or moral responsibility. This is not a country or a society where youngsters can or are expected to support themselves, although in dysfunctional families they are sometimes forced to try. This is a time when little children and adolescents alike must depend on others, usually their parents.

During adolescence, neglected young people may attempt to run away, feeling unwanted and searching for the thing that is missing in their lives. However, such escape may lead to prostitution, drugs, crime, or worse. Social service or law enforcement agencies may locate the teenager and return her or him to the same dysfunctional home. Many others never have the nerve to leave, realizing that the alternatives they face on their own may be far less pleasant than a known situation in which they've learned how to survive.

This existing dominant social system may work fine for healthy families, where age is no indication of a person's value in the family and where respect for each individual's worth is honored. But in patriarchal systems these families are the exception, not the rule.

When the System Fails, Children Suffer

When parents are abusive or simply have no time for or interest in their children, the system fails. There are few other safe places for children to turn, and those that do exist are frequently unacceptable. Foster homes and institutions may be as damaging, neglectful, or abusive as the family of origin.

If neglect occurs when youngsters are still forming their identities, the damage is severe. In the process of learning who we are as individuals, we believe ourselves to be the image that we see reflected back in the eyes of those around us. The first and most important of these belong to our parents, the adults who provide for us and make our world.

Children of neglect see little good in their parents' eyes. Rather than seeing love or hate, they see nothing. It may be as though no one is looking back. The adults' neglect tells the children they are, at best, unimportant. Their self-esteem sinks lower and lower as they wait for attention.

Youngsters who are neglected have no language to describe the kind of shame that comes from silent rejection. That shame is a feeling that makes people question if they are worthy of love. It is an intensely powerful shame born of the break between ourselves and the adults who give us our identity.

Having those all-powerful parents turn away from us as children hurts horribly. The pain can hit just as hard whether it's from running up for a hug and being ignored or from waiting expectantly for a new outfit and being tossed a worn hand-me-down, knowing the money was spent on alcohol. It's the feeling attributed to the "poor little rich girl" whose parents provide her with every toy and every social or educational advantage, but are never around to get to know their child. It isn't an injury children can easily name, such as a sore finger, but it's there all the same. They know something's wrong, something's missing, but they don't have the language or experience to say what that is.

This kind of hurt isn't visible like a bruise. Still, it is real. Consider Sarah, a troubled adolescent whose problems were far deeper than anyone realized:

As far as her parents knew, Sarah was a shy, introverted but intelligent child. She never missed a day of school and spent a lot of time in her room, even when her family was home. As an only child, Sarah knew she was lonely, but that wasn't all she felt.

Until she began school her parents had kept her close at hand. She socialized only with her parents' adult friends and held fast to her mother's skirts at birthday parties and company picnics. She was scared to death of other children.

It wasn't that Sarah's parents meant to neglect her. Her bedroom was furnished with an elaborate canopy bed chosen from a catalog. She proudly displayed the latest in dolls and a library of children's books. She always went along on business trips or vacations. Sometimes the trips even included places just for her, like Disney World.

Still, Sarah wasn't happy. Her parents told her she was spoiled, that she had everything a little girl could possibly want. Sarah believed them, of course. She decided there was something wrong inside her and if she could only be good enough she could "fix" it. If only she were good enough, she could make her parents love her and fill the empty spot.

Soon, Sarah became the star of the fifth grade. She wrote the class play, brought home the best report card, even placed at the county track meed. When the empty spot bothered her, she just tried harder.

By high school, Sarah's low self-esteem and self-hatred were well established. She ran from herself constantly, joining every club, running for class offices, signing up for the most difficult academic classes, trying out for sports teams. She continued to excel, gaining crumbs of external self-esteem when she'd occasionally overhear one of her parents tell a friend about their daughter's accomplishments. But that only made her work harder and run faster in search of more tidbits of acknowledgment. She never learned to love herself.

Eventually, Sarah's race for reward wore her out. She met a young man who seemed to love her in a new way. He was sincere when he held her and talked about their future together as they planned matching careers and a family. Sarah felt hope, yet she didn't believe she deserved his love. Her feelings of self-hatred were rewarded on the occasional times when her boyfriend didn't meet one of his goals. Filled with anger, he drank too much.

If Sarah complained or refused to let him drive home, he grabbed her. The beatings scared her at first, but he was always sorry the next day. And somehow, the physical abuse eased the emotional pain inside her. It confirmed her feelings of worthlessness, leaving her worn out but with less tension and stress. She could finally relax, finally allow her feelings to drain out in physical pain.

As an older teenager, Sarah knew enough to hide the fighting from her parents. What's more, she didn't believe they would care. She expected they would feel obligated to do something—to call his parents, to report him to the police, to forbid her to see him—but she know they still wouldn't ask about her feelings. Sarah was fighting her own battles and she wasn't about to share.

By the time the child reaches adolescence, such parental neglect can be a direct route to delinquency and other troubles. Without ever feeling good about themselves at home, teenagers turn to their peers for status. Without the security of a positive self-image, they fall into trouble. They repeat the patterns of their parents. Just as their parents failed to take care of them as children, they neglect themselves as teenagers and young adults.

Neglectful Parents Miss Something

Neglectful parents have many of the same characteristics as physically abusive parents. These adults are isolated, irresponsible, immature, and have trouble controlling their impulses. However, there are some differences in behavior. While abusive parents are somewhat compulsive and clean, neglectful parents don't adhere to routines.

Preoccupied with meeting their own needs, they may be unable to recognize and meet their children's needs. They may fail to see that their son's pants are far too tight or recognize that their daughter's poor grades come from poor vision. They don't know their children's teachers. They fail to show up for dancing recitals or soccer games. Of course, not every parent can make every event, but the neglectful parent usually has something else that takes priority. Their children get last place. They may try to deny this fact to themselves and to others by justifying the time spent working or doing other things, but the children get the message. By adolescence they usually give up even asking.

Neglectful parents may be experts at escaping from responsibility or reality. They may abuse alcohol or drugs, hiding from themselves and their children. They may become workaholics, spending their children's lifetimes at the office. They may become addicted to other behaviors that occupy all their time, keeping them focused on themselves and their obsession rather than on the young people who need them so desperately.

A history of deviant behavior frequently foreshadows the tendency to be a neglectful parent. Teenage fathers can actually disappear, deny their connection to the child and escape responsibility in other ways. A teenage delinquent who becomes pregnant and accepts motherhood may never have experienced actively loving parents. If she was already involved in problem behaviors before she gave birth, she will most likely continue those patterns. Becoming a parent probably won't change her, and the baby faces almost certain neglect.

The immaturity that forms the character of neglectful parents gives them childlike demeanors. They themselves may throw temper tantrums, having food fights or going off to pout in a corner rather than fixing a nutritious dinner for a hungry child. By adolescence, teenagers may act more mature than the parents themselves, taking on caretaker roles and responsibilities. Other young people model themselves after their immature parents, coping with stress through addictions or the same childlike behavior they see at home.

Isolation Reinforces Inattention to Family

Parents who have no time for or interest in their children are also likely to be isolated from community resources. Parenting programs require participation. Help from social services comes only when one inquires and then is willing to spend considerable effort contacting the right person or meeting the exact specifications for qualifying. When family is not the priority, children can be neglected, and parents remain wrapped up in the other parts of their lives.

Parents who neglect their youngsters may do so because they have physical or psychological ailments that have nothing to do with the amount of love and concern they have for the children. When parents are blinded by physical pain from genuine medical problems, they may see no choice but to expect their children to be so self-sufficient they begin to feel neglected. Other parents may be so emotionally unbalanced that they can't see what they're doing to their children. They may be preoccupied with imagined illnesses or personal needs so that the children end up being ignored.

Some parents may be genuinely emotionally or mentally ill, yet have never been diagnosed or received treatment. Children, even adolescents, have little on which to base a comparison of behavior. They may not know it isn't normal for Mother to spend every Saturday compulsively cleaning the same closet. They may not realize healthy adults are consistent in their choices and responses, thinking it perfectly normal that Dad wakes up cheerful but goes into a rage at the same suggestion that made him laugh the day before. These youngsters may even think these episodes or the irrational behavior depends on themselves, that they're the cause, and therefore they must fix the problem.

Neglectful parents have a poor sense of responsibility. They fail to realize or care about the seriousness of rescinding a promise to take their high school senior to the class picnic. For the parents, the decision was never final. They are living for the moment. For teenagers, the event is of monumental importance. Missing it might seriously damage their social standing with their peers, something that matters even more because neglected young people may gain much needed self-esteem from their friends. To have their parents care so little about what's important to them doubles the negative impact and cuts the adolescent's self-esteem to shreds.

A low energy level is also characteristic of parents who neglect their children. They may work hard all day or they may drown their health in a bottle of wine. Either way, when the children come home from school and it's time for family activities, the parents may feel like doing little more than collapsing in front of the television. If they are faced with preparing supper, doing housework, and other chores as well, they may never find the strength to show interest in the children's homework or activities. By the teenage years, young people are well aware of their parents' feelings and may never even mention what's going on with their lives. These are the same parents who fail to supervise their adolescent's activities or to know their friends.

It is common for these parents to face personal conflict in their own lives as well. They are constantly processing their pain, their childhood abuse or neglect, their religious rules versus desires. They may never have the time to see their children's needs because they are so wrapped up in their inner struggles.

Financial needs can cause even conscientious parents to neglect children. The single mother whose three jobs keep her off welfare and keep her children fed may have no choice in the amount of time she is available. If she can't afford quality day-care and is forced to place older children in a latchkey situation without supervision, neglect is the obvious result. Not all neglectful parents would choose their lifestyles, but other issues (such as lack of community resources) may keep them down.

Neglectful Parents Find Safety in Numbers

Neglectful parents sometimes have a support group— assorted friends or merely acquaintances who share the same values. These other adults probably also neglect their children and share common beliefs and characteristics with each other. In fact, these families are often aware of being outcasts from the community around them, and so they withdraw from others. They don't visit other people or invite others to their homes. The result is little feedback on housekeeping or child rearing.

This lifestyle isn't new to the parents. Frequently they themselves grew up in poverty. Chances are they were neglected by their family of origin and had little example to follow. They learned inadequate parenting skills through example, yet felt no one outside their family cared about them either. When they carry over into adulthood this lack of understanding about parental leadership, feelings of alienation, and mistrust of outsiders, they continue the trend with their own children.

Another common trait is an extremely negative attitude, believing the worst of any situation and always looking at the darker side. In their interactions with other adults, they experience few positive moments.

Naturally, their interactions with their children follow this negative pattern. Rarely do they give their children compliments, finding fault rather than encouraging good behavior or accomplishments through praise. They are more likely to respond to children when things get out of hand and punishment seems necessary than when the youngsters are well-behaved. They are also less likely to do fun things with their children, expecting them to be "seen and not heard."

These parents expect much of their children. They have many requests, expecting youngsters—especially adolescents—to do as they're told including chores and responsibilities. Still, the parents don't go out of their way to help the children, or to make special concessions. They won't be the folks who drive the Brownies to camp every other weekend. They're the ones whose little girl wears the wrinkled dress because either she always does her own ironing or nothing gets ironed at all.

Familiar Patterns Can Be Recognized

All these behaviors may not be evident in any one neglectful family. Each group of individuals has its own dynamics, its own character. However, there are three patterns that repeatedly emerge in the development of both abuse and neglect, which originate from similar sources.

Unrealistic Expectations. The first pattern noticeable in abusive and neglectful families begins in childhood. In fact, chances are the parents themselves experienced similar neglectful or abusive treatment when they were children. It is a dysfunctional generational legacy, but one that can be changed.

Abuse that begins early in the children's lives usually happens because parents have unrealistic ideas about what they can expect from youngsters. As a result, the children have low self-esteem and the family grows isolated. Fearing failure, the immature adults feel inadequate as parents. They appear dependent, domineering, disorganized, and overwhelmed by life.

Neglect beginning in childhood is characteristic of families that are chaotic and disordered. Family members have trouble coping with day-to-day life. Parents frequently play the role usually taken by the oldest sibling, competing with the children to get their dependency needs met. When their attempts fail and their needs go unmet, the youngsters in these families learn to believe that other people are unreliable.

Children see themselves as the center of their world, so when their parents let them down they blame themselves. This begins with low self-esteem, developmental lags, or signs of behavior disorders. The youngster begins to feel unwanted, unloved, flawed, or worthless. These feelings expand to the community, school and world about them. The result is a feeling of debilitating shame that increases the child's sense of insecurity, lack of self-respect and powerlessness.

Control Issues. In the second pattern of abuse, the quality of punishment changes when the children reach adolescence. Corporal punishment is still accepted in society as an appropriate method of discipline regardless of its effectiveness. Spankings and other forms of physical punishment are often used in childhood.

As the youngster reaches adolescence, however, corporal punishment may become less effective. Lacking leadership skills, parents depend on power to control their youths. They increase the amount or harshness of punishment.

Different religious, ethnic, or racial backgrounds also can affect the degree of physical discipline used. For Afro-American families, discipline is one of the most significant variables affecting their lives. This legacy of Afro-American discipline can be traced back to slavery, when children had to be trained to be compliant and obedient to avoid

71

harsh, often cruel punishment. Racism and the realities of today's world continue a situation where the best-disciplined Afro-Americans are the ones who escape crippling problems such as teenage pregnancy, poor education, drug and alcohol addiction, crime, unemployment and welfare dependency. For many black families, this means keeping their young people in line with strong physical punishment. Stress, poverty, and culturally reinforced poor self-esteem hurt black families as they attempt to find themselves in today's society.

Similar conditions affect other groups. Single mothers may overcompensate for the lack of a partner by extreme forcefulness in discipline. Other families may have learned abusive or neglectful behavior that in other countries or societies are seen as appropriate.

As the teen years approach, conflict also emerges between the parent and youth, disrupting their normal routines. The resulting anger and frustration may lead to an increase in corporal punishment from that used in childhood. If it becomes harsh enough, it changes from culturally accepted physical discipline to abuse.

Parents feel they are losing control when confronted by adolescents' quest for independence. Not being able to keep up with the youths' development from being children yesterday to teenagers today, they fail to understand why young people need to explore separation and test issues of control.

As their ability to control their children is threatened, parents become more strict. Their fear of losing control results in adolescents who cannot internalize values or develop self-control. Self-esteem sinks lower for these youths, and problems develop in school as they act out their feelings. Juvenile delinquency frequently results.

In families where neglect begins in adolescence, developmental issues of control are also at the root of the problem. Rather than exhibiting overreaction of abusive parents, these adults "give up" their parental responsibilities. They feel they can no longer manage or discipline their adolescents because they fail to understand how the youths are changing and testing their boundaries. They fail to understand who owns the problems, stepping in when their youngsters should be problem solving and tightening reins that should be loosened.

Finally, the neglectful parents refuse to participate in problem solving at all. They may have been unsuccessful at taking over their children's lives, so they quit trying to parent at all. Their feelings change from a desire to nurture their teenagers to a need to "protect" themselves from the feeling of failure.

Approaching Sexuality. The third type of adolescent abuse or neglect involves a variety of family factors. As adolescents' sexuality begin to develop, relationships change between parents and children, and incest issues may arise or become more severe. Possessive or dependent parents may have problems dealing with the maturing teenagers' needs for more independence. Separation problems take on a new relevance. At the same time, parents may be forced to confront issues they didn't resolve during their own adolescence.

73

Families in which parents have previously indulged their children are most likely to fall into this type of pattern. Dependency and compliance are routine and expected. Anger and frustration arise when the adolescent begins to seek independence, an unanticipated change.

Similarly, this pattern of neglect during adolescence happens when the emotional or intellectual development of the parents conflicts with the growth of their children. Issues of the adults' lives are brought home as their youngsters mature. These parents react to their own life crises and withdraw from the youth. The teenagers find themselves suddenly alone with their problems and without a leader to help them find their direction. Rather than too much discipline, these youths have too little.

Because they don't feel successful at adult leadership with their adolescents, neglectful parents resort to doing nothing.

Summary

Neglect happens in families where the parents are too preoccupied, too insecure or too ineffective to provide positive, interactive leadership roles. Some parents may not care about their children at all, having taken on family responsibilities unwillingly or before they were ready. Others were abused or neglected themselves as youngsters, so they have no knowledge of what a healthy family is like or what they need to be doing to be active, effective parents.

There may be physical, emotional, practical or financial reasons that neglectful parents fail to provide the kind of support their children need, especially as the youngsters reach adolescence. In fact, this coming-of-age may be a pivotal time when the adults fear they are losing what control they have and the youths are striving for independence from an unhappy home life. Parents of teenagers may be shocked at the behavior of their offspring, causing some to turn to abuse and others to abandon parental responsibility.

While attention turns to those youngsters who are physically or emotionally battered, those who suffer from neglect cannot be forgotten. This is the breeding ground for as many social problems as abuse, an increasingly serious issue that society cannot afford to ignore any more than parents can afford to ignore their children.

5

Why Do They Hurt Me?
Causes of Adolescent Abuse

Why? Some victims of abuse spend their entire lives trying to answer that one question. They wonder what they did to deserve such treatment, mistakenly assuming the blame for another's angry lashing out. They repeatedly examine their behavior, questioning how they could change; what they could do differently to keep the abuser from striking.

There may be no single answer. Abuse has many causes, and it certainly can't be prevented by the victim. That was true for Perry, a young man whose father's alcoholism contributed to his abusive behavior:

"He would come home and he would be blasted out. We would be sitting and he would walk in and look fine. I could tell he was drunk though. And I kept thinking a lot of things in my head because he would start screaming about a lot of things.

"Last summer we got in a fight and he threw the food at me and I got up and left. I went upstairs crying and listening to him yell at my stepmother.

"If we did something wrong at my uncle's house, he would come home drunk. My dad would line us up. He had a belt and he would beat us with it.

"I was pretty young. I was six or seven years old. He did that until I was thirteen-years-old, almost every weekend."

Severe physical punishment seldom equals the seriousness of the children's perceived misbehavior. For Perry, this became a regular part of his family life.

"If we did something minor, he would make it into something big. Maybe if I got caught chewing snuff in the house and before I got to say anything he would say, 'I want to talk to you.' He would take me into the basement and start beating me. He would always kick my little brother in the behind.

"He would kick me like that, and he would be just out of his mind. He would kick us up the steps. He threw me down the steps.

"We were fighting the whole way up the steps. He was punching me and slapping me around. I just couldn't take it and I started hitting him back.

"He just looked at me. He thought it was just a big joke. He made the comment, 'You shouldn't have done that and you know what you are going to get now?' He just picked me up and threw me down the steps. I just got up and was crying. I didn't know what to do.

"He just kicked me back up the steps and I was laying in my room for hours. Then he would come up and my mouth would be bleeding and my lip would be all cut up. He would try to say he was sorry."

There are many causes of adolescent abuse, usually occurring in combinations. They range from alcoholism to family stress to personal issues.

Perry's father clearly had a chemical addiction problem that influenced his abusive behavior. Even the boy was aware enough to see that the man beating him was "out of his mind." But the fact his father isn't sober or acting out of rational thought doesn't erase the damage done to this trusting child.

Of course, there are people who never drink but still beat their children. And there are alcoholics who would never, ever use violence. These are just strands of the complicated webbing that produces parents who abuse the special children they created.

Like Perry's father, these parents may not realize how extreme their behavior is until after the abuse has been done. They may feel sorry. They may try to make up for the children's pain by buying presents or offering special privileges. What they can't do is change what has happened.

TOO OLD TO CRY

How Can They Do It?

Why do these parents lose control? What malfunction, what misconception causes parents to make such tragic mistakes?

Stress is a major culprit. Today's world is one of fast-paced change and demands. Career, financial obligations, and personal demands compete with picture-perfect television success stories. Money buys less. Fast-track employers demand more. Religious institutions tighten their restrictions and demand obedience. Yesterday's luxuries become today's necessities, and society gives a clear message to those who find it difficult to reject materialistic values.

Stress itself is complex, stemming from many possible causes. External stressors have to do with the state of the world and the situation of the specific family. They prey on the vulnerability of the adults and magnify personal issues. Finances, social relationships, geographic mobility, education, and poverty all play a role.

Coping with unwanted pregnancies or social isolation are the kinds of interpersonal problems considered internal stressors. They can also be caused by children with serious behavior problems or with special needs caused by illnesses or handicaps. Any disruption that happens among family members can increase stress and make dysfunction more likely.

All families must cope with stress. In fact, stress keeps people going and life interesting. It's when the stress becomes overwhelming, when the family can no longer bear up under constant pressure, that abuse can happen.

Teenagers Create New Challenges for Families

The developmental issues of adolescence create extreme stressors for a family. Teenage changes affect the parents as well as the youngsters. Adults who are not expecting or prepared for transitional behaviors may find the stress of coping with teenagers more than they can handle.

Although there are plenty of myths about the problems with rearing teenagers, families are still surprised. Youths' behavior during these years may be seen as provocative and erratic. Parents fail to understand that teenagers experience frequent mood swings. They have trouble coping with the adolescents' need to test their parents' control and authority.

At this point in life, youths are experiencing the world through new behaviors. Part of doing this is seeking separation and independence from their family.

Adolescence is also a time of personal growth. Teenagers are concerned with their feelings, behaviors and beliefs. They are developing their individuality, and their identity, and testing their new roles.

At this time of personal awakening, adolescents have boundless energy to plan their futures and fall in love. They usually have a very positive outlook on life. Their days are exciting and hold much promise.

81

Problems arise, however, when their parents' view of the world also changes, differing greatly from that of their idealistic youngsters. Adults who have raised their families to the teenage years have reached their "midelescence." They feel less energy instead of more. Marital problems are common at this stage. Symptoms of menopause for mothers may be occurring. For males there is the mid-life crisis. This means these parents typically spend more time assessing their accomplishments than planning their futures. Their eyes are on the past and present, while their children are looking into the future.

It's not surprising that the challenges of "midelescence" oppose the tasks of adolescence. When parents are un-prepared or find it too difficult to cope, they may find themselves depressed or over-stressed. These feelings can be a natural part of developmental growth. However, these feelings of depression and stress decrease the parents' tolerance for the teenagers' emerging vitality. In the abusive family, the parents' intolerance may lead to lashing out and abuse.

During adolescence, teenagers are starting to think and reason more like adults. They develop the ability to deal with hypothetical problems and think abstractly. The change is usually welcome, but conflicts can arise when parents realize these new abilities will be applied to activities outside the home rather than with primary focus on the family unit.

At the same time, youths are rarely as self-confident as adults. They don't trust their own intuition, so they look to the role models around them. They may imitate adults who seem to the teenager to be competent. They assume the views, opinions, and even behaviors of these individuals.

Abused Teens Learn to Model Their Parents' Behaviors

Adolescents from healthy families have plenty of positive role models from which they can choose. Children of abusive or neglectful families also may look to their parents or adult caretakers as examples, not realizing there are other options or modes of behavior.

Perry talks about the way his abusive, alcoholic father influenced his behavior:

"My stepmother and my mom always said that I wanted to be like my dad, which was true. He started to smoke, so I smoked. I was about eight years old. He was drinking. I saw that. I grew up with that, so I started drinking. That led me into a lot more things. My dad doesn't do drugs, but he drinks and alcohol is a drug.

"I was in rehab last summer and if I didn't live with my mom they were going to put me in a foster home if my mom wouldn't take me. I was clean for six months and now I started using again.

"Then my dad tried to tell me he had changed. In the first two weeks, we were friends. Then he told me he had changed, he had quit drinking. The week he got home, my stepmother left him. I heard from my aunts, cousins, everyone that he is drunk. He told me he wasn't drunk.

Basically, he is lying to me a lot. Sometimes I feel like calling him up and I start swearing at him. But I feel sorry for my dad and don't want to say anything to him."

Despite suffering abuse, Perry found himself copying his father's behavior. His family's influence was overwhelming.

During the teenage years, however, young people are exposed to adults in a variety of ways. They are not limited to copying family members when they begin to assume behaviors and values. They get to know teachers, coaches, and other outsiders to the family unit. They watch television and movies. They can read magazines, newspapers, and books. Through today's communication networks they are exposed to a variety of choices. They learn about positive and negative alternatives in lifestyle, politics, religion, and education.

As teenagers begin to imitate singers, movie stars, or sports figures, parents may be shocked at their children's behavior. They may not choose to live with the habits of a rock star, the ego of a teen idol, or the toughness of a football hero. Young people know these role models as the image on the screen, not as whole persons. Without personal knowledge of the individuals, they can copy only those aspects of their personalities of which they are aware. Parents may have a difficult time dealing with these replicas in their homes so conflict arises. If these adults resent the fact their children haven't chosen to emulate them, the conflict may be even more difficult.

If teenagers choose positive, strong role models in their family or community or in the media, the results may be good. One of the world's most successful blind athletes, Craig McFarlane, has taken cross-country tours offering himself and his accomplishments as an example of what a young person can do despite difficulties. Accidentally blinded at the age of two, he went on to international fame in wrestling, water skiing and track. He helped carry the torch for the Olympics when they were held in the United States, and he has spoken at the national Republican convention. Several years ago he began direct outreach to young people by sending himself on tour to schools where he could let teenagers know it is possible to surpass the odds.

McFarlane, however, had an extremely supportive family. They insisted he learn mobility, raising him to handle himself and his chores on their Canadian farm. He was sent to a school for the blind during grade school, but his parents removed him when the institution refused to let him participate in sports. They insisted McFarlane be mainstreamed into public schools where he could compete on the wrestling team. He became a champion, a positive reinforcement of his abilities and his self-esteem that led him to outstanding achievements in life.

This is the success story of an adolescent raised in a healthy family. McFarlane had enough belief in himself and enough support from his parents to overcome his perceived physical limitations. He understands about role models and beating the odds. That's the message he wants to inspire in other youths.

Youths Accept What They're Used To

There is a sadder side to peer pressure and role model-ing, however. Children from abusive or neglectful families are exceptionally susceptible to negative influence because it is all they know. When they see outrageous or illegal things done by famous personalities, teenagers are likely to think the behavior is okay. They believe if their movie idols can get away with it, then they themselves should be able to. They glamorize destructive behavior. They mistakenly connect the star's success with their dysfunctional activities.

The results can be worse than obnoxious behavior or petty theft. An increase in teenage suicides has led re-searchers to believe that people are more likely to kill themselves if there has been a suicide in their family. Individuals who are already contemplating suicide may be encouraged to kill themselves when they hear about the successful suicide of a person they know, like, or admire. When the person is another adolescent, peer identification is strong.

The same holds true when the suicide victim is a celeb-rity. Teens identify so closely with popular media or entertainment figures that news of their suicides may bring the youths closer to making their own attempt. Any glamorization of the death by schools, the media, or the community especially affects those who are fragile and vulnerable. Their injured self-esteem and topsy-turvy value system perceives the notoriety as recognition and special attention that was obtained through suicide. The reality of death may never register. Instead, these emotionally needy young people see the commotion as a very appealing response.

Parents, especially those distanced by their abuse or neglect, may be totally unaware of this negative development in their children. Along with intellectual changes, adolescents are developing socially outside the family structure. They spend much of their time with peers. Often these friendships compete with family relationships, having as much or more influence than parents. It happens at the very time youths are struggling with parental values and peer demands.

Even as the youths are looking outside the family for relationships and for role models, the world's social atmosphere is constantly changing. Behavior or dress that was acceptable when today's parents were young may seem tame compared to current fashions and trends. In the late 1960s, a boy might be admired by peers but expelled from school for being brave enough to grow long hair. That same boy would suffer extreme humiliation if he then dared wear an earring, although today's young men may tie their identity to such jewelry. An interracial teenage couple in the early 1970s would likely have found themselves excluded from social life and restricted from contact by their parents. Today, having a romantic friend of another race may go unnoticed or even be held up as an example of social progress. A gay college student may think twice about taking another male to the school's homecoming dance, but twenty years ago the two wouldn't even have been allowed in the door. In fact, they probably would have been expelled.

Changes in societal values affect both adults and adolescents. Parents and other family members may be taking on new status in their own lives and in the eyes of their children. Whether the adults go along with the changes in society or cling to archaic values, teenagers are likely to do just the opposite of whatever their parents choose.

It is common for adolescents to begin to view their parents as untrustworthy outsiders or intruders in their young lives. The polarization is more than a generation gap. Youths and adults separate themselves from one another, contributing to the growing feeling of mistrust. It is a part of growth.

Dysfunctional Parents and Teens Isolate Themselves

Isolation frequently follows in dysfunctional families. Instead of coping with the changes and accepting the developmental patterns of their youngsters as a normal part of the growing up process, parents may feel they are failing. They grasp for control or give up completely. Some parents isolate themselves and their families from others, preventing their children from having any significant social relationships.

The children aren't the only ones suffering from isolation. Parents who choose this way of dealing with adolescents will themselves avoid community or school activities. They distrust people, feeling threatened by outsiders and uncomfortable with their own differences, lifestyles, or abilities.

During their children's teenage years, they can no longer completely control this separation from society. Adolescents are developing friendships with others. They want to take part in school-related activities and have enough mobility to do so, in spite of the fact their parents may try to prevent it.

Parents who don't actively take steps to keep their youths at home and away from the world may still resent their youngsters' attempts at outreach. They may tell them so, or they may act out their feelings in inappropriate ways, causing the teenagers to feel guilty or shameful, even when making their own reasonable choices. Stress and conflict result. Enough pressure or ineffective coping within the family unit eventually evolves into overt adolescent abuse or neglect.

Summary

The pressures and stress of the teenage years are sometimes enough to cause parents to abuse or neglect their youngsters for the first time. Even adolescents who were obedient and nearly perfect as young children begin to question their family's values and lifestyle and begin to seek unique identities. This can be a greater challenge than youths or adults can meet. Parents often find their children reaching the teenage years at the same time they themselves are experiencing a mid-life crisis. This developmental clash can cause the family relationship to deteriorate.

Teenagers who are getting to know themselves will test out behaviors they learned from role models. They copy parents, movie stars and others they admire. They reach outside the family, making new friends or getting involved in new interests. When these choices don't please their parents, the adults turn to abuse or neglect out of frustration.

6

What Happens After?
Effects of Abuse and Neglect

Nothing happens in isolation. If a parent beats one child, she will probably hit another. If a parent forces incest on one child, he will probably rape another.

The same is true for behaviors. If a parent gets drunk once, she probably will drink again. If a parent uses violence as harsh discipline, he probably will strike out again.

Abusive or neglectful patterns don't happen just once. They occur as early as infancy or as late as adolescence. Chances are these patterns are rooted in the parents' ancestry and that they will continue within their offspring —unless recovery begins; unless someone, somewhere along the way, wakes up and blows the proverbial whistle. If that person is the abuser and is willing to find help, then the pattern may stop or be changed. But every day that person's family participated in dysfunctional behavior—

whether as the cause or the reactor—was another day those destructive patterns were reinforced.

The effect is similar to the ripples that follow a rock thrown into a pond. The rock sinks to the bottom immediately after impact, but the surface of the water continues to ripple in broadening, widening circles. The more rocks, the more violent and the more frequent the waves.

For the family disturbed by the impact of destructive behavior, the ripples of the first rock barely subside before a second and a third disrupt the surface calm of the family relationship. Before long, children and adults alike learn that to survive they must cooperate with the waves or the disruption. Few individuals are strong enough or aware enough to learn to swim away. Instead, they begin to believe that constant upheaval is the norm. They learn abnormal or dysfunctional behaviors to survive.

Family Members Don't Realize What's Wrong

These patterns may involve physical abuse, or they may be limited to emotional abuse and neglect. Whatever the dysfunction, chances are that most of the family members have no more than a vague awareness of what may be wrong. Young children especially are unaware that life can be any different.

Mark, who has two chemically dependent parents and an alcoholic grandfather, only began to realize that his family was different between the ages of nine and thirteen. Even when he tells his story of severe abuse and neglect, he contradicts himself. No one wants to believe their family doesn't work, that their family is dysfunctional or worse.

Mark's story is a clear example of the perception of an abused adolescent:

"I always thought other families were perfect, that they didn't argue or anything. It was always my family, always my mom. (I thought that) no other families on our block did this.

"I was always getting into fights with my dad and beat. I thought that was all that ever went on until a couple of years ago, when I was maybe twelve. I started to hang out with girls and started to meet their parents. Her parents were really nice. I said to myself, 'Wait a minute. This ain't what it is like in my house.'

"I had the worst family in the neighborhood. I would go to my friends' house and see how their parents acted. There was this one house I went to and the kid was only nine years old and was cussing his mom out. I thought, 'My, what's going on here? I thought my family was the only family in the neighborhood with problems.' But I saw some other families with it too.

"I lived in a fantasy. Wishing, I pretended a lot in school, pretending there were no problems but all the kids in school knew it wasn't like that. I knew it wasn't like that. They knew what my mom was like and I would try to hide it a lot and try to live in a fantasy life. Watch Leave It to Beaver and hope that's what it is like."

The Fantasy Family Lives On

This great ability to create and believe in the ideal family fantasy is one reason that it is so difficult to tell if an adolescent lives in an abusive or neglectful family situation. Young children, totally dependent on their parents, twist their view of reality rather than believe the worst about the adults they both need and love. They take the blame on themselves. They make up great imaginary scenarios rather than acknowledge the truth. By the time they reach adolescence, they believe the fantasies themselves. They may be in total denial of reality, and they may be too ashamed of their real family and themselves to admit the truth even to themselves.

When an outsider challenges or simply questions youths' fantasy families, the teenagers feel threatened. They want to believe their concept of reality. They want to believe their parents love them and that their family is as normal as Beaver Cleaver's. They fear change as much as they may fear the constant abuse or neglect. That's why it is so difficult to determine the true situation by asking an adolescent. Even if the youth knows the truth, he or she will seldom admit it. They may be protecting their fantasy or their parents. They may be afraid to tell for fear of repercussions at home. They may not trust any adult, especially one outside the family circle.

The only way to detect the truth about whether an adolescent is being abused or neglected may be by careful observation over time.

Look For Physical Signs

The most immediate and visible effect of abuse and neglect is physical damage. The broken bones, bruises, and lacerations commonly found in young children who were abused are not as evident in adolescents. The teenager's size and ability for self-defense can limit the extent of physical injuries that occur.

Even a large youth may be unable to conceal the signs of abuse if a weapon has been used. This can happen especially when the abusive parents view their adolescent as harder to control. When they resort to the use of a weapon, there is generally apparent physical damage. However, getting the youngster to admit the real cause of the injury may be difficult.

The great lengths to which adolescents may go to protect their parents testifies to the far-reaching effects of growing up in an abusive or neglectful household. What begins as a physical injury leads to less visible problems later.

Physically abused children frequently show delays in development, learning disorders, motor disorders, or mental retardation. Other times such treatment at home results in hearing loss or poor physical growth.

Emotional Signs Signal Warning

Victims of abuse and neglect may show any or all of numerous symptoms of maladjustment. These include low self-esteem, high anxiety, lack of empathy, suicidal tendencies, aggressive behavior, alcohol use, school and social adjustment problems, delinquency, acting out, running away, inhibition, withdrawal, fear or wariness of adults.

Often the myriad of symptoms combine into a condition known as codependency. People raised in addictive or dysfunctional homes, victims of abuse and neglect, and family members of addicted or compulsive individuals all are susceptible to codependency. It is so prevalent today that groups such as Codependents Anonymous are spreading across the country to help those who identify with the symptoms. Based on the Twelve-Step principles that originated in Alcoholic Anonymous, these self-help groups encourage recovery and an understanding of what healthy relationships are about.

Children raised in dysfunctional homes, even those not blatantly abusive or neglectful, don't even know there is a name for the behavior patterns that pervade their lives. The term codependency was first used to identify partners or family members living with alcoholics or addicts.

Recent developments in understanding the personality and symptoms of the codependent show that the condition may exist even in people who have never known a chemically addicted person. A more current definition of codependency is offered by Melody Beattie in her book, *Codependent No More:* "A codependent person is one who has let another person's behavior affect him or her, and who is obsessed with controlling that person's behavior."

Just as individuals, many of whom are parents, can act compulsively and addictively in many ways (workaholics, food disorders, exercise addicts, and so on), so can co-dependents develop in a variety of family structures. Relationships that are out-of-balance produce lives that are out-of-balance. This happens in abusive families, where the victims feel locked in dysfunctional relationships and can find no "justifiable" way to help themselves.

Adolescents Need Alternatives

Children are even more susceptible to this way of thinking. There may truly be no way for juveniles to help themselves as long as they are limited by their age and education. They may want to escape, but not realize there is any alternative to dysfunctional living. They may wonder why they don't run away, then feel shame that they have stayed with their family and allowed themselves to be abused. They may believe everything was fine before they were born, and therefore they must be the problem. They feel responsible for their parents' abusive or neglectful behavior, and may, in fact, be blamed for the situation by their parents.

Control becomes an issue for powerless children when they feel they are at fault and that they must "fix" the family or the dysfunctional adults. By adolescence, most youths have perfected a mode of behavior in response to the family's problems. They attempt to control their feelings and their behavior. They attempt to control their parents' actions by behaving in ways they believe will elicit the desired response. They manipulate rather than directly approach any situation.

There is no blame, however. Young children and teen-agers cannot "fix" their parents. But that doesn't stop them from trying.

Part of the atmosphere that encourages codependency is prolonged exposure to a set of oppressive rules. These rules prevent open expression of feelings or direct discussion of personal and interpersonal problems. These are the rules abused or neglected adolescents have learned well. It is how they survived.

Abuse and Neglect Hurt Self-Esteem

Abuse and neglect leave children feeling worthless. They believe they are disliked by others, including their families. They fear that their actions displease others and therefore they must be responsible for and deserve the abuse.

These young people are totally unaware that they have no control over the fact they are being abused or over the behavior that caused the abuse. For many adults and children alike, their codependence can be so strong that, when degrading or destructive things happen to them, they can't see the acts as negative. It isn't that they think about them as positive; they just don't think about them at all. Their codependency keeps them from asking for help because they are afraid to ask, feel isolated, or are unsure that something really is wrong. They have such low self-esteem that they don't think they are worthy of intervention.

Anxiety is closely related to self-esteem. Victims tend to think of themselves as unworthy. Not trusting themselves, they become dependent on the opinions of others for feelings of self-worth and identity. For teenagers, this may mean their parents or any of the other external role models available. They take on others' values and behaviors because they believe others are better than they are. Since they make decisions and act based on external sources rather than their intuition or judgment, these adolescents are constantly anxious about whatever they say or do. It is vitally important that people think the best of them, because it is from these external sources that they get any self-esteem they may have.

Feeling overly dependent on others for this reassurance of self-worth, abused youths lack empathy. Empathy is the ability to understand how another person is feeling.

Learning About Empathy

An abusive home does not provide a warm, caring environment in which empathy is allowed to develop. Abused children don't experience empathy from their parents or other family members once they all become numb due to constant hurt and conflict. Instead, the home environment teaches pain and anguish, which in turn causes family members to develop insensitivity to pain. This is how these young people survive.

A lack of empathy, low self-esteem, high anxiety, and aggressive behavior leads to poor social relationships. Adolescents in these circumstances have not learned how to interact with others. They have no skills for communicating their feelings or needs to others. Isolation results,

99

even when the teenager doesn't withdraw from or fear others. At the base of this is mistrust, which thwarts the development of any close personal relationships.

It isn't that adolescents don't see some glimmer of something different in the world around them. By the teenage years they might yearn for healthy relationships— or at least for an experience where they are not just the victim. When support is missing at home, youths will look for it in other places. They may not know how. They may not know exactly what it is they want. But that doesn't stop them from looking.

This often means running away, taking to the streets where they feel they at least have some control over their choices. Some teenagers may try to escape through more acceptable forms of compulsive behavior, such as becoming absorbed in school work or athletics. That doesn't make the adolescent any healthier, only headed in a different but similarly unfulfilling direction.

Hurting Teens Look For Escape Routes

Other techniques for escaping from the hurt of an abusive, neglectful, or dysfunctional home are drinking, drugs, and suicide. Abused teenagers drink more than non-abused teenagers. Their alcoholic adventure can be an attempt to forget or relieve their pain, frustrations, or feelings of powerlessness. Drugs may be used for the same reasons.

Suicide is a more permanent, definite way of escaping from the pain of being abused. The adolescent may feel there is no other way to end the abuse; that the only way out is suicide.

More than one thousand teenagers a day are attempting suicide, a drastic increase over the last twenty years when the general suicide rate has remained constant. Eighteen of those one thousand adolescents who attempt suicide are successful, meaning that every ninety minutes a young person dies at his or her own hands.

A suicide attempt is often a cry for help or a way for youths to tell parents they are still dependent on them and need them to meet their needs. Other causes may be failure, loss of a love object, rejection, and depression. Societal influences include lacking stable emotional or family roots, having personal identity crises regarding issues such as sex roles, perceiving the need to succeed or fearing failure, feeling pressure to grow up too soon, or other demands.

Alcohol and drugs become interwoven with suicide attempts because adolescents are tempted to use them to reduce anxiety and psychological pain. Chemicals reduce inhibitions, allowing the teenager to express more easily anger and unhappiness through suicide. The desire to escape by killing oneself is magnified, while the false bravado due to the chemical influence gives the youths temporary and false security for coping with their problems. When they learn no new way of dealing with their problems, despite the temporary euphoria of alcohol or drugs, the young people are even more vulnerable to suicide.

Delinquents Act Out Their Feelings

Delinquency, the lack of conscious effort to meet obligations, is also related to adolescent abuse. It happens when youths act out their feelings, run away, skip school, and steal or engage in other crimes.

When delinquent behaviors are considered in relation to the environment of the abusive family, it is clear that:

1. Abuse victims display predelinquency traits;

2. Both abuse and delinquency arise from common environments; and

3. Abuse and aggression go hand in hand.

The high levels of fear and anxiety that adolescents feel because of abuse and neglect are often expressed as acting-out behavior. Unable to speak about their needs or feelings directly, they attempt to manipulate others. They don't know how to ask to have their needs met, so they try to get others to take care of them. And since they can't verbalize their needs, they may fear they'll be deserted.

Anxiety also may come from feeling shame about themselves, the debilitating shame that's the root of their inability to act constructively in their own interests. If they further act out the fear by running away, they are more likely to experience violence in the streets and later, in the home, if they are returned by authorities.

Again, adolescents who find themselves in these circumstances almost always learned their behavior at home, from the actions of their parents and other adults. Abused teenagers, who lack the interpersonal and problem-solving skills to handle routine situations in life, imitate their parents' coping strategies. Those youths who choose to model after or identify with the abusive adult are the same ones who seem predisposed toward crime or delinquency.

Typically, physical abuse and neglect produce children who continue to lose confidence in themselves, their abilities, and their coping methods. It isn't surprising that they mistrust others, particularly adults. The extent to which they have incorporated these feelings and behavior depends on the duration, extent, and severity of the abuse. The age of the child at the time of the abuse and the nature of the injuries also affects adolescents' dysfunction.

Abused Teens Survive by Learning to Cope

Victims of abuse have several ways of coping with stress. The three most typical tactics are caretaking, hiding, or provoking.

Abuse victims may assume the caretaker role to cope with the fear of their parents' abuse. Adolescents try to avoid abuse by being "good" and keeping the household running smoothly. They take on codependent characteristics as they step into a role reversal with their parents. They grow up quickly, becoming the functional adults in the family but without real power or adequate preparation. As victims, they deny their feelings and try to meet their parents' needs instead of their own.

Sometimes victims want to hide or disappear when their parents become angry. They learn to withdraw into themselves, keeping their distance from adults or other family members. It is a behavior that can carry over into true adulthood, increasing personal isolation despite friends or family.

Victims of abuse sometimes equate their punishment with love. They provoke attack because they desperately want to feel loved. They purposefully anger their parents, setting the stage for abusive treatment. Soon they know the limits of what they can do to trigger the parents to punish them. They learn to manipulate against their own best interests because their value systems are as dysfunctional as the family with which they live.

Whatever the reasons adults abuse their children of any age, there is no justification for such behavior. No one causes himself or herself to be physically abused, and that includes children or adolescents. Regardless of what the youths may believe about themselves and their ability to control their parents' behavior, adults must be responsible for themselves. They are the only ones who can create change. Their children and their spouses cannot "fix" or rescue them.

Summary

Destructive patterns happen over and over again in abusive and neglectful families. Set in motion perhaps generations before, the dysfunctional behaviors are learned through role modeling and personal experience as youngsters learn to cope in whatever way possible. Some children try to "fix" the family problems by exceptional behavior and by caretaking. Others choose escape routes by running away, turning to addiction or even committing suicide. Many delinquents are simply acting out feelings they could never express.

The only way to stop the cycle of adolescent abuse and neglect is to intervene. Rarely do parents recognize themselves as abusers, although they themselves may be victims of their own low self-esteem or dysfunctional behavior. More often, interruption comes from outsiders such as teachers or law enforcement officers.

7

Recognizing The Danger Signs of Abuse

Susan is a quiet child who volunteers little in class. Her teacher is surprised one day to notice a long, narrow bruise down the back of the girl's leg.

Maybe that's why this sullen teenager's always so withdrawn. I'll bet there's abuse at home, the teacher thinks.

She recalls Susan's unhappiness about her parents' recent divorce. The teacher promises herself she'll look into this further, but when questioned, Susan offers little more than a shrug. The teacher's suspicion increases.

Craig, on the other hand, always shows up at school with odd marks, even on his face at times. The teacher says nothing, questions nothing. He's a big kid. She knows he plays football.

Had this teacher investigated further, she might have been surprised by the truth. Quiet Susan got her marks from gymnastics—a fall on the balance beam. But Craig, despite his size, played football more as a cover-up for injuries than because of his bulk. He'd never dare raise a hand to his father, an alcoholic with an abusive temper.

Just as in these hypothetical cases, things are not always as they seem. This is especially true when it comes to reporting child abuse.

Abuse Means Getting Hurt

An abused or neglected child is one "whose physical or mental health or welfare is harmed or threatened with harm by the acts or omission of (acts on the part of) the child's parents or other person responsible for the child's welfare."

This broad definition applies to many different kinds of behaviors, environments, and their consequences. Its open-ended nature both protects the victim and makes detection and prosecution difficult. Determining when a child should be considered abused or neglected may therefore be the greatest challenge facing those concerned about the youngster's welfare.

Physical signs aren't as easy to recognize as we might think, especially in the case of adolescents who are aware of the legal consequences of their parents' actions. They may love or hate their abuser, but they will often stop short of reporting their caretaker when they know it could break up the family and land the adults in jail. Seemingly plausible explanations are offered when these teenagers are questioned, making confirmation of true abuse even harder.

Technically, physical abuse is "nonaccidental injury inflicted on a child by his or her parents or caretaker." This includes such violent acts as hitting, throwing, kicking, or burning the youngster. It is most easily recognized by studying observable injuries the youthful victim receives.

Look For Common Physical Signs

Those concerned about abused children and adolescents should watch for these common signs of physical abuse:

- Bruises, especially those of multiple colors (green, yellow, blue or black) that indicate stages of healing

- Bruises in shapes suggesting an object was used (wire, cords, hand)

- Bruises to several parts of the body

- Bruises around the head

- Burns

- Complaints of soreness or awkward movements

- Extreme sensitivity to pain

- Bald spots suggesting hair pulling

- Bone fractures

- Lacerations

- Frequent abdominal pain or swelling

Watching for such physical evidence is only the first step, but with practice at careful observation you can learn to recognize suspicious injuries or patterns of injury.

All youngsters get bruises, even adolescents. Their youthful abundance of energy and willingness to engage in rough activities frequently cause casual injuries that show up the next day. That's why it's so important to know what you're watching for and if there is a pattern or discernible mark visible.

Weapons Leave Distinctive Marks

Bruises and lacerations from abusive treatment often take the shape of the object used to inflict the injury. These are termed pattern wounds or bruises. For example, a loop-shaped wound usually suggests that a cord, doubled over, made the injury. A bruise or welt that wraps itself around the body is a clue that a flexible object, such as a belt, was used.

When you're looking for a sign, watch for marks that reflect the exact nature of the instrument involved. If you find the angular impression of a corner or a specific shape, the odds are that abuse occurred. If ropes are used, even the weave of the fibers may be visible. Anything can become a weapon in the hands of an abuser.

Burns, especially those intentionally inflicted, also take the shape of the object or weapon. Those that are glove shaped, usually on the hands and feet, suggest that immersion in a hot liquid occurred.

Any scars or marks that indicate specific weapons or types of injuries should be questioned. The youth may lie or give an implausible response to a direct inquiry, but even this answer should be evaluated. Does his or her explanation make sense to you? Have you noticed similar marks on the child at other times? Does he or she speak with sincerity or do you sense a cover-up?

Once you have determined or believe you know the source of the injury, you have a place to begin. However, this is only the start of your investigation.

Child abuse may be the first and most obvious cause of injury, but remember that adolescents encounter a variety of adults and peers in many situations daily. Injuries alone may not be evidence that abuse has occurred. Fights with other juveniles, rough play in an athletic sport, or a legitimate accident may have caused the suspicious-looking mark. Don't jump to conclusions.

Believe in Common Sense

Your own common sense or intuition about a particular child or situation may be your best guide when evaluating

111

possible abuse or neglect. At the same time, it is vital that you dismiss any stereotypes or preconceived ideas you may have about which families abuse or what kinds of youths are inclined to become victims. Violence can occur in any type of family and at any socioeconomic level.

Some trends, however, are evident. One study of physically abused youths showed "younger children and females were more likely to be victimized by an implement."

The use of weapons is not uncommon in cases of adolescent abuse, especially in families where previous, milder forms of discipline were not working. Believing they needed to be more powerful than the teenager to control their child and "make" the child behave, these parents may be desperately seeking methods with which to attain that control. They subscribe to the philosophy that they must use whatever works to keep their child in check, even if it means inflicting pain.

Adolescent Victims Won't Talk About Abuse

Some teenagers will choose to remain silent about abuse at all costs, preferring to protect their parents and remaining loyal to the abuser. Others, having been conditioned to accept the abuse, allow themselves to be beaten rather than fight back.

Low self-esteem contributes to the victimization of abused adolescents. Some of these children have never seen how the functional, nonabusive family functions. They don't know there is a choice or that they actually have a right to stop the abuse themselves. They may even believe they deserve the beatings.

The fresher the injury, the more likely you are to determine its cause. Health care professionals, law enforcement officers and others who often see children immediately following abuse can gain additional information about the problem by observing both the youngster and the adult caretaker.

On the other hand, because of the size and self-defense abilities of adolescents, they may show none of the obvious physical signs of abuse. Their behavior may, in fact, be the only indicator that something is wrong.

If you become involved in the situation early enough, you will want to look for patterns of behavior that clearly suggest abusive treatment. Typical responses can be observed in the adolescent victim and also in the parent or custodial adult.

According to the Florida Department of Law Enforcement's guidelines in the *Florida Juvenile Handbook*, the following behaviors offer clues to the source of injury:

PHYSICAL EVIDENCE:

CHILD'S BEHAVIOR:

Bruises, Welts
Burns
Fractures
Lacerations
Genital area

Cries Hopelessly
Wary of Adult Contact
"Poker Face" (Somber)
Watchfulness
Suspicious

ADULT'S BEHAVIOR:

Stressful Relationships
Acute Tension
Unreasonable Discipline
Impulsive Actions
Unreal Expectations

If you suspect that a child or teenager is being abused, but the youngster refuses to divulge information, you can still watch for behavior that is characteristic of victims. Combined with physical clues and accurate information about the youth's home life, these symptoms usually indicate a dysfunctional or abusive family.

Behavioral Clues Point to Abuse

Specific behavioral signs you'll want to notice when seeking to verify possible physical abuse include:

- Exaggerated response to being touched

- Provocative actions that attempt to push others to the limit of maltreatment

- Extreme behaviors (aggressive or withdrawn)

- Assaulting behavior

- Inappropriate dress for the weather (hiding visible evidence of abuse)

- Fear of parents or other adults

- Acting out (incorrigible behavior)

- Overcompliant attitude

- Destruction to self and others

- Inability to form good peer relationships

- Alertness to danger

- Frequent mood swings

There are particular behaviors to watch for in middle school, junior high and high school students. According to the Florida Department of Health and Rehabilitative Services, younger teenagers will act out extremes. They may appear too aggressive or may totally withdraw from social interaction. They may be frightened of their parents and afraid to go home, although they may actually report injuries inflicted by their parents.

If sexual abuse is involved, these youths are often unwilling to change for gym or to participate in physical education. They frequently withdraw from situations, have poor peer relationships, and are reported as delinquents or runaways. They may seem bizarre or too sophisticated, or they may display unusual sexual behavior or knowledge. Eventually some of them do report sexual assault by a care-taker.

Victims aged eight to sixteen are often underachievers who seem to have no strong moral or spiritual values. They seek attention, affection, rewards, praise, and approval. They have more money in their pockets than is usual for their age. Frequent appearance of new toys and new clothes may be cause for suspicion.

It is also valid to check into how the youngsters spend their days or evenings. Abused youths commonly spend more than the normal amount of time at recreation areas and hangouts or in the company of adults. Usually they are withdrawn from family and friends, forming new peer groups.

Make No Assumptions: Actions Can be Misleading

Of course, not every child who acts in these ways is being physically abused. That's what makes detection so difficult and reporting so serious.

Most adolescents display some of these behaviors at one time or another. While these patterns are likely to suggest an abusive situation, the same responses can be symptoms of other problems or even reflect differences in cultural or ethnic backgrounds.

While most authority figures charged with assessing child abuse cases are white, middle-class professionals, families reported for abuse are disproportionately drawn from the less educated, the poor, and ethnic minorities. Black children are overrepresented as victims of abuse, while whites are underrepresented in reported cases of maltreatment.

These statistics tell us who is most often reported for child abuse, not who is more likely to commit acts of violence against juveniles. An additional study by Hampton showed that there is a much higher incidence rate of abuse among low-income families than in wealthier households, a finding certainly related to stress.

Financial Status Makes a Difference

Interestingly, the study also tells us that while blacks and whites have equal and low rates of maltreatment among affluent families, low-income whites have significantly higher rates of child abuse than do their black counterparts. As a result of this finding, Hampton suggests "ethnic differences in child maltreatment are small when all groups have adequate socioeconomic resources and larger when groups experience impoverishment."

Mexican-Americans were found to have the lowest rates for abuse and for abuse and neglect, although not for neglect alone, according to Hampton. When comparing frequency of types of maltreatment within ethnic groups, Anglo-Saxon families showed the highest proportion of abuse. Mexican-Americans and blacks had a greater proportion of neglect. Hampton concluded that cultural factors influence these differences.

"The lower abuse rates among Mexican-Americans suggest 'less manifest aggression and violence toward children,' which may reflect socialization patterns producing a 'more passively and internally oriented style of coping with problems and challenges of life' and a personality type that is 'more accepting of life's conditions and perhaps less aggressive in interpersonal relations.'"

Although other minorities are frequently overlooked, their customs and tendencies toward violence also should be noted. In a study of Japanese-Americans and Samoan-Americans, the more affluent Japanese-Americans were much less likely to abuse their children but were more prone to neglect than their poorer counterparts.

Non-Anglo cultures also must be recognized as practicing customs unfamiliar to white, middle-class Americans. Vietnamese children, for example, may suffer from bruises around the head and neck due to the use of common remedies for headaches and colds.

Don't Buy Into Ethnic, Racial or Other Stereotypes

What we learn from these cross-cultural observations is not to trust any stereotypical assumptions. A family's economic status may tell you more about its tendency toward abuse than may its racial, ethnic, or cultural heritage. Assumptions based on the background of the observer cannot be made if the investigation is to be valid.

The implications of such an error in judgment can be severe. A mistaken accusation may have ramifications that are just as detrimental to the accused as the abuse is to the victim. All factors must be heavily weighed before you report a suspected abuser to authorities. Even when you are certain there is abuse going on, you may be unable to point a finger directly at the offender.

To complicate further the task of investigating suspicious cases, children and teenagers are likely to refuse to cooperate with you. This is true regardless of the potential for change.

It takes great bravery for an adolescent to name his or her abuser, especially if the person is a parent or family member. If sexual abuse is involved as well, the youth may be hesitant because he or she may feel some responsibility for the act.

False Accusations Can Destroy Lives

At the same time, there are occasions when teenagers use poor judgment in blaming adults for abuse that never happened or that was done by someone else. A false accusation of abuse, especially child abuse and assault, can destroy the life of an adult so any action should not be taken lightly.

Ed Hartmann, a Florida school bus driver, nearly died of the stress he suffered after three adolescent girls falsely accused him of sexual assault. Labeled a child molester, his photo was widely published after his arrest.

Amazed at the accusation when confronted by Pasco County Sheriff's officials, the sixty-year-old Hartmann thought it was all a misunderstanding. No bail was set when he was arrested. Believing that, since he was innocent, he would be out the next day, he delayed hiring an attorney.

Two months later, still behind bars, Hartmann suffered health problems. After open-heart surgery and a hospital transfer followed by cardiac arrest when he almost died, his case finally came to trial. Hartmann spent his family's entire savings on his defense.

There was little satisfaction when the judge threw the case out of court because he discovered the girls testified to the grand jury that Hartmann had done nothing to them at all. The bus driver believes the teenagers were angry that he made them sit down on his bus.

The Hartmanns later sued the school board to pay for Ed's legal expenses, but money won't erase the stigma that still surrounds the family or the health risks that resulted.

Investigation is the key. Perhaps authorities acted too quickly in the Hartmann case, yet in other incidents little or no action results when abuse is plainly evident. That's when an unrelated person may provide the intervention that makes the difference for the abused adolescent.

Heavy Caseloads Impede Investigations

There is plenty of domestic violence for law enforcement and social agencies to deal with. Heavy caseloads prevent adequate evaluations. Repeated calls to police that aren't backed up with legal action give officers little chance to make a difference.

Continued police action did little to help Jesse, an adolescent whose addictive and abusive mother always abused her.

In Jesse's words, "I was always scared to do something about it. I would run and hide from her and the cops would come because her and her boyfriend would be fighting and I would hide in the bathtub or anywhere I could. I was always afraid to be there.

"My brother, Charles, and me, the humiliation she put us through. Like the cops would have to come and drag us out of the house. All the neighbors would stand outside and look at us. It was humiliating. Our house got robbed one night. The cops came. She finally got us back a week later and she went out and got drunk and she blamed that on us.

"When I turned about twelve or thirteen, I started to get tired of getting beat around, hit around. I started to run away a lot. The last time the cops brought me back to my house she was drunk and she went off on me. I went to bed that night and she came in and stabbed me with a screwdriver. After that I just left. I couldn't handle it any more."

If you observe any of the typical characteristics of abuse in a teenager, your first move should be a search for additional evidence. You may later conclude there is good reason to suspect an abusive situation, or you may see other complicated reasons for the dysfunctional behavior. Find out as much as possible about the child and his or her family and home conditions, before making a final judgment.

At the same time, it is vital that abusive families such as Jesse's not be overlooked. The boundary line between suspicion and knowledge may be a fine one, but in some cases determining the truth of a situation requires risking investigation.

The key to identifying abuse rather than simply dysfunctional behavior or accidental injury lies in the reason given when the adolescent is questioned. Often his or her report of how the injury was received does not justify the type or extent of the wound.

Again, study any physical marks. Be sure the stated cause matches the evidence. For instance, when a bruise bears witness that the youngster was hit with a flexible object, don't accept football as an explanation.

Evaluate the Suspected Abusers

If you can't determine the validity of your suspicions of abuse from the child's behavior or from the physical signs, you will want to consider evaluating the parents or custodial adults. Most abusers have common traits or personality characteristics that are identifiable.

Abusive parents are often very critical of the child. They live socially isolated and have unrealistic expectations of the youth. They may not interact effectively with the youngster or with others around them.

Eleven family dynamics to consider when attempting to identify abuse or neglect cases are:

1. The parents' personal and marital problems

2. Parents with a history of poor relationships with their own parents

3. Parents who were abused themselves as children

4. Parents who were raised in a home where excessive punishment was common

5. A family that is isolated, transient or lacks external support systems

6. Parents who are evasive and contradictory in explaining anything about the family situation

7. A family with little or no interest in the child's treatment

8. Parents who constantly criticize the child and blame the child for the injuries

9. Parents who have inappropriate expectations of the child

10. Parents who dislike the child or act accusatory or judgmental

11. Family members who seem to have no acceptable outlet for their pent-up emotions

Again, many of these characteristics may be present in families that do not abuse their children. That's why serious investigation is necessary.

Look for other confirming indicators before reporting suspected child abuse. If physical harm is involved, note any contradictory history given by the parent. Listen for a story that fails to explain the type and extent of the injury. Also, find out if there is a history of abuse in the family or in the parents' families.

Protect Yourself With Backup Support

Even when you've checked all the indicators and are convinced that child abuse is going on, it is wise to consult another person for backup. Unless danger is imminent, you provide yourself with a margin of error by enlisting the aid of another unrelated adult who is familiar with the adolescent and his or her family situation.

This step may be more for your own protection in case you are challenged than for the sake of the suspected victim. However, it is not unreasonable to look for support since few abusive families will welcome your interest.

Still, when all the results are in and the verdict is clear, reporting child abuse may be the greatest favor you can do for the young victim.

Summary

Identifying abuse isn't as easy as it might seem, especially with adolescents who refuse to talk about it. The first confirmation of child-battering can be seen in physical marks. There are common signs that can be identified when examining injuries. There are also attitudes and behavior patterns that can suggest such problems exist at home.

Reporting the abuse to authorities can be the only way to help the victims, but it is vital that outsiders making accusations be absolutely certain that the charge is valid. This is not something to be taken lightly, and it pays for the person making the complaint to have backup testimony. Taking steps to help the abused teenager may be a risky endeavor, but when the mental health and physical well-being of a youth are at risk, it must be done.

8

Subtle Symptoms
Spotting Neglect

Neglected children show no bruises or scars to indicate the pain they experience daily. They cannot name their oppressor, for they have no understanding of what they should be able to expect from their parents.

The experience of neglect may be the most confusing. It takes many forms and affects individuals in many dimensions. Yet, in a society where action is prized and passivity left to occur in a void, little attention is given to the child who is emotionally injured. In the world, as at home, no one notices.

One definition of neglect is "the failure of the child's parents or caretakers, who have the material resources to do so, to provide minimally adequate care in the area of health, nutrition, shelter, education, supervision or attention and protection." To this list one must add emotional, psychic, and spiritual care, although those parents who neglect on physical levels are likely unable to have the resources to nurture themselves in these additional areas.

Identifying Common Forms of Neglect

There are six commonly identified forms of neglect:

1. *Educational neglect* is the failure of the parent to provide for the educational development of the child.

In these families, social isolation is so great that the parents do not allow the children to attend school. No alternative education, even home schooling, is provided.

Even where the youngsters are sent to school, the parents show no interest in education-related activities. Report cards and notes home are ignored. School functions are not attended, and the parents fail even to meet their children's teachers.

As the parents show no interest in education, many children soon adopt their parents' values. They may become chronically truant, never caring about missing school and never truly connecting to the learning process. They develop learning problems, making it even more difficult to identify with school or to value education.

Eventually these young people withdraw from the group. They are the dropouts, the teenagers who quit school as early as possible because they don't fit in or because they never learned what it was about in the first place. They are also likely to have intellectual, social, or personal development problems.

2. *Emotional neglect* occurs when the parents fail to provide the love, affection, and security a child needs.

Emotionally neglected children are more difficult to identify. They are often adequately dressed and fed, sometimes in the tradition of the "poor little rich girl." They may come from wealthy, poor, or middle-class homes. They may be only children or one of many. It is the absence of any physical sign that makes detection difficult.

Behavior, however, offers a clue. Emotionally neglected youth may actively seek-out others who will acknowledge their existence. They are emotionally needy. They also may suffer from developmental lags or be mentally disturbed.

This form of neglect involves more than merely ignoring the children. Emotional neglect may involve verbal abuse such as belittling, degrading, slanderous remarks, or threats of harm. It develops a keen sense of shame in the youngsters.

Some neglectful parents use confinement as a form of discipline or out of ignorance. They restrict the youngsters' movements by literally tying them down or by locking them in a room or closet. These methods give parents control they cannot gain through active leadership because they have no skills, are ignorant about effective parenting, or simply don't care.

3. *Physical neglect* occurs when parents fail to provide adequate clothing, food, shelter, or supervision.

These youngsters are easier to spot. They are chronically hungry, show poor hygiene habits, and may have inadequate clothing for the weather. These physically neglected youths are usually outcasts because of their poor hygiene and their lack of knowledge of acceptable social behavior.

4. *Abandonment* happens when parents leave their children alone for long periods of time or leave them inadequately supervised.

Parents of young children may do this by leaving little ones alone in the house, car, or bedroom for extended periods of time. As they get older, these are the adolescents who find themselves responsible for a family of younger siblings when they themselves are still at a young age. A nine-year-old is far too young to be responsible for a houseful of younger children, especially into nighttime hours, but this is exactly what neglectful parents will do.

In the most severe cases, parents completely reject the children. They may actually disappear, leaving the youngsters to fend for themselves, or they may simply ignore the existence of their offspring as much as possible. Either way, the lack of care makes a deep, long-lasting scar on the youngsters.

5. *Nutritional neglect* is the failure of the parents to provide an adequate diet for the child.

Severe cases of nutritional neglect result in malnutrition and are medically observable. Although school systems are making some effort to speak to this need through free lunches and food programs for school children, these parents do nothing to provide a proper diet for their children. This form of neglect also sets the youth up for poor lifetime eating habits, leading toward obesity or food disorders.

6. *Medical neglect* occurs when the parents don't provide adequate medical treatment for suspected or diagnosed physical conditions.

This type of neglect is aggravated by a social structure where good medical care requires the ability to pay, to have adequate insurance, or to have the endurance and knowledge to work the public health system. Dental and optical care are part of the parcel, although these aspects are frequently more neglected than traditional medical needs.

If the parents themselves have never had proper medical care, they may be unaware that they are neglecting the children's welfare. Many school systems offer health screenings as preventive measures, but those who are truly neglected may already be missing school and unavailable for testing. They are the ones who complain of ailments or who continually appear ill but show up anyway.

7. *Spiritual neglect* may never be detected or listed in conventional abuse literature. Families who are struggling to put food on the table, to keep their children healthy and to provide adequate housing

will seldom consider spiritual needs to be an important area. Yet, when addictive or compulsive individuals begin recovery from these afflictions, they conventionally turn to Twelve-Step programs that are based in self-defined spiritual connection.

Organized religion may have no relationship at all to spiritual wholeness. This is a quality of life that requires personal experience of a deep power that everyone at whatever age must define for themselves. Children or youths who are missing this quality of life may see little to hope for beyond mere survival.

Adolescent Neglect Sets Patterns for Adulthood

All of these aspects of neglect, and more, are detrimental to the development of the adolescent. Neglected teenagers are used to a life lacking in routine and organization. It is a pattern that they carry over into later life and probably pass on to their children.

Neglected youths usually lack the ability to organize. They appear to have poor hygiene habits and should be easily spotted, but they often bypass intervention by dropping out of school, leaving home, or turning to crime.

There are physical signs that can help identify neglected youngsters:

- Torn, dirty clothing

- Ill-fitting clothes

- Inadequate clothing for the weather

- Constant hunger

- Always seeming tired

- Poor hygiene

- Unattended medical needs

- Delayed growth and development

Neglected adolescents also may show none of these characteristics. In fact, they may deny that they are neglected out of protection of their fantasy family. Because they must depend on their parents for love and support, they don't want to believe their parents aren't caring adequately for them. Therefore, neglect, like physical abuse, is more likely to be detected by noting emotional or behavioral indicators.

Neglected Teens Feel Worthless

Teenagers who suffer from neglect feel they are of little value and treat themselves accordingly. Their personal experience has taught them to be mistrustful, and not to believe what people say. Their needs have not been met in the past, so they have no reason to believe they will be cared for in the future.

Youths in this condition are often indifferent and passive, lacking enthusiasm for life or activities. They haven't

133

learned to talk about their needs or feelings. They are emotionally immature and may not even be aware of what their needs or feelings are.

Other emotional indicators that teenagers suffer from neglect include:

- Low self-esteem

- Reluctance to enjoy activities

- Apathy

- Withdrawal, shyness

- Isolation from others

- Immature social skills

- Delayed social development

- Dependency usually characteristic of younger children

The age of the children when the parents first began to neglect them plays an important role in determining how the adolescents will act out their feelings. If neglect started early in life, the children may change dramatically when adolescence sets in. If they identify with an abusive parent or if they harbor great anger at their parents' lack of concern, they may replace withdrawal or shyness with aggression.

Emotional indicators must be observed by watching a youth's personality. Patterns and values must be understood in context.

Common Behaviors Are Rooted in Neglect

There are certain behavioral characteristics common to neglected children:

- Poor social relations

- Truancy

- Vandalism, theft

- Alcohol or drug misuse or abuse

- Aggression

- Withdrawal

- Destructiveness without guilt

Also, neglected youths are frequently rejected by their peers. Reasons involve the way the adolescents look, smell, or act—problems the youngster developed precisely because of being neglected.

This rejection from their peer group keeps neglected youths from being able to develop physical or emotional bonds with other teenagers. So, they suffer from delayed social development, and others consider the neglected adolescent as "babyish."

Indeed, these young people are often immature and childish. They may show signs of dependency that others their age have long ago left behind. They may cling to anyone who shows them a little love or affection, but also will reattach to the next person who offers warmth.

There are qualities of adolescent neglect that are very different from childhood neglect, whether the omission occurred from infancy or just began in adolescence.

Parents May Give Up At Adolescence

Family conflicts resulting from developmental issues may lead to neglect that starts during the teenage years. Parents may feel they can no longer control the youths, so they give up their responsibilities as parents.

In these situations, the parents and children are vying for control. The adults fear they are losing control, which they are. Rather than seeing adolescents as nearing a time when they can make their own decisions and reap the consequences, these parents withdraw rather than face disappointment or failure. Eventually, they neglect the youth altogether.

Situational factors also may cause parents to neglect adolescents. As the parents react to their own mid-life crises, they focus less and less on the children. Through no fault of the teenager, the adults withdraw and the youngsters face neglect at a time when they need their parents' guidance the most.

Adolescents learn to mask their feelings. They act out inappropriate behaviors rather than acknowledge their pain. Abused youths may divert attention from their parents' neglect by dropping out of school, turning to juvenile delinquency, running away, manipulation, or stealing. They may become involved with the juvenile justice system through these behaviors long before the abuse or neglect is discovered. Even when they become identified by the system as juvenile offenders, they may so effectively hide the nature of their home environment that their maltreatment goes undetected.

Child abuse and neglect is usually discovered through physical signs or behaviors of the young victim. With adolescents, abuse and neglect often remain undetected until a violent outburst occurs. The family or strangers may be involved, but the abuse may be discovered by law enforcement officers, social workers, teachers, or neighbors.

Sometimes the Truth Isn't Enough

Just knowing the youth has been abused or neglected does not mean that proper intervention will occur. Not all people in positions of authority have an understanding of the effects of abuse or neglect on a child or adolescent. Some professionals or other adults may fail to understand the root of the problems. They may blame the youngster for the assault. They may believe swift and strong punishment is the only deterrent to the youth's violent behavior.

This misconception occurs when adults fail to connect the patterns of behaviors taught to abused or neglected children through the actions of their parents. Because of their size, mobility, and ability to avoid conflict, teenagers are often seen as able to take care of themselves. They are expected to know the difference between right and wrong, despite whatever values their parents showed them.

The system fails when these characteristics are not associated with cases of child abuse and neglect. The result is that the adolescent is not seen as a victim and therefore not treated with compassion.

The truth is that many cases of adolescent abuse are very different from the situation of an abused young child. Teenage cases seem more representative of the general population, while child abuse or neglect occurs more frequently in high-risk groups. These include single parents and the poor.

Youths Learn to Solve Problems With Violence

Children and adolescents whose mothers are battered are more likely to be physically abused themselves.

Partly this happens when abusive men use the same tactics to control their children that they use to try to control "their" women. Even if the youths have not themselves been battered, they may have developed certain characteristics that show they have been caught in the "crossfire" of an abusive relationship.

These youngsters have learned to use violence to solve problems with other children and family members. They get into fights at school. They hit first and question motives later.

At the same time, youths who have witnessed or experience abuse tend to blame themselves for things that go wrong. They take on the codependent feelings of responsibility and self-blaming.

Adolescents who have witnessed abuse at home have poor impulse control. Just as their parents are unable to maintain healthy emotional balance, these youngsters are unable to put off immediate gratification. They also may have learned that if they wait for something to happen, it won't.

They don't understand the dynamics of violence. Without any healthy comparison, they assume abuse or neglect is normal and occurs in all households. When they create families, they frequently follow in their parents' footsteps, becoming abusers or victims, depending on how they identify themselves.

These teenagers feel isolated from their peers because they are embarrassed about their home situation. When they do realize their family is atypical or unhealthy, they hide the reality from others and often from themselves.

Personal Boundaries are Unclear

What may appear as lack of respect is actually the adolescents' failure to understand personal boundaries. They may easily violate others' privacy or choices, unaware that they are getting too close or overstepping their bounds.

Abused or neglected teens tend to lash out at others. Although they themselves may be experiencing extreme shame, they deal with it by blaming others for their problems.

Family secrets are clearly related to abuse or neglect. By adolescence youngsters are well aware of what may safely be disclosed and what information must be kept quiet at all costs. They know the price of exposure and fear reprisal.

If the father is the abuser in the family, the youths may blame the mother for his behavior. Just as they may see themselves as responsible for their maltreatment rather than as the victim or survivor, the teenagers hope that their mother will come to their defense and stop the father's violence.

The adolescents also may blame themselves for their father's actions. They may feel they should be controlling the situation; that if they only behaved better or kept the household calm then he would stop.

Teens from these households frequently exhibit jittery behavior. They are jumpy, restless, or easily startled. Youths who witness or suffer abuse at home may spend time daydreaming about how they can beat their parents when they get old enough or big enough to stand up to them. Other signs of emotional maladjustment include:

• Low self-esteem, a poor self-image, and lack of confidence are constant companions for abused or neglected teenagers.

• These youths show anger at everything and everybody, especially their mothers.

• Hyperactivity or excitable behaviors can be expected to occur among abused or neglected youths.

• These teens are unaccustomed to limit-setting. They don't know when to stop even if told, because nothing at home is stable. Rules seem made for breaking, not for respecting.

• Abused or neglected youths are unable to recognize, label, or express feelings appropriately or at all. This is why acting out and manipulating are so common.

• Extremes are the norm. These adolescents tend to appear happy one moment and angry the next.

• Those adolescents who have routinely watched their father beat their mother may vow never to hit a woman, yet end up battering just like their dad.

Emotional abuse is the constant companion to physical abuse and neglect.

TOO OLD TO CRY

Individual Adolescents React Differently

These signs, of course, will not appear in all children from abusive or neglectful families. While some of them will develop behavior problems and stay in trouble, others will become incredibly compliant. They may appear fine on the outside, but their inner selves are in constant turmoil. They are terrified to express their feelings.

Adolescent abuse and neglect may well involve more interpersonal problems than child abuse and neglect. While children deal with life on a base level, teenagers experience more interaction with the world and community outside the home. They are more mobile and more independent, although still dependent on their parents for basics. The reactions and characteristics they have may reveal the quality of their socioeconomic and demographic life more than their ability to handle a dysfunctional situation.

This is why adolescent abuse and neglect survivors need to be considered differently from child victims. The pain is no less serious and no less debilitating; but it is different.

Summary

Although neglected adolescents are harder to spot, they are no less vulnerable than abused teens. Their parents aren't there for them in many ways, causing them to feel worthless and unloved. They find themselves without support for educational development, emotional needs, and physical necessities. These teens lack adult guidance and supervision. Other needs that may be neglected include nutrition, medical care, and spiritual fulfillment.

Certain behavioral and emotional signs are common among neglected youths. The older the children are when the maltreatment begins, the better adjusted the teenagers will be. However, by adolescence most youngsters know how to conceal their feelings and how to hide their home problems. They keep family secrets and mistrust adults. They internalize what they've learned through experience, making them likely to repeat the neglectful patterns in their adulthoods. It is because they themselves are so close to stepping into grownup roles that makes intervention in adolescent neglect so important to society.

9

What's Being Done
Coping With the Problem

Isolation may be a key symptom of abusive and neglectful families, but in today's world it's nearly impossible for
anyone to be totally alone. Children go to schools, usually
public, where they interact with other youngsters of various
races, cultural heritages, and family lifestyles. Adults work,
usually for a business or organization that employs others.
Except in a few truly desolate areas of the country, everyone has neighbors.

A late night domestic fight next door will most likely
wake up your baby. A lost drunk looking for home at 2:00
A.M. could well lean against the closest doorbell—yours.
Your child's favorite playmate at school may have an
alcoholic parent whose problem you don't discover until
after your youngster has visited their home.

Dysfunctional families are the majority in this country.
It is unlikely, even if you live in the healthiest household

on your block, that you or someone in your family will go without being somewhat affected by someone from a dysfunctional home. And chances are that problem family will be at least once touched by abuse or neglect.

That's why adolescent abuse and neglect isn't just somebody else's problem. It doesn't belong just to the neighbors down the street or that family you heard about at the community center. The teenagers who are victims of that abuse or neglect are your children's friend, your children's baby-sitter, or the juvenile delinquent who robbed the corner convenience store.

One day those adolescents will be adults. They'll be our in-laws, our attorneys, our health-care workers or the parents next door who abuse their own kids. If we don't act now to do what we can to stop this epidemic of abusive, neglectful, and dysfunctional families, we'll have to deal with the consequences later.

Adolescent abuse and neglect are everyone's problem, and that includes the community as a whole. Those affected by this epidemic include people and agencies involved in protecting victims, particularly law enforcement and social service organizations supported by tax dollars.

Currently, legal, medical, psychological, and social networks are responding to the problem on a community basis. Still, each of these networks can only do so much. They play only a small role in intervening in and preventing adolescent abuse and neglect. The rest is up to us.

There are several ways public and private agencies deal with this social problem. Each approach has different benefits. Some methods work best in certain places or with particular kinds of families; others are more effective under other circumstances. Where the concerned citizen should turn when reporting possible family maltreatment or when willing to become part of the solution depends on the situation and the services available.

Child Protection Team Provides Collective Support

Many communities speak to the problem of domestic abuse, neglect, and violence with a multidisciplinary child protection team. The benefit of this approach is that the troubled family can draw from the expertise and energy of a variety of individuals. Working together, a group of professionals assesses, investigates and treats victims of abuse and neglect. This makes it possible for decisions to involve input from a variety of viewpoints, including that of social workers, educators, juvenile justice workers, therapists, law enforcement officers, medical professionals, and volunteers familiar with community service.

Child protection teams are usually designed to respond to the particular needs of the local community. The professionals live, work, and participate in the same town as the clients, giving them firsthand knowledge of the predominant lifestyles, economic factors and even the weather. Among the services customarily provided are identifying abused and neglected children, verifying and diagnosing cases, treating the family and the victim and educating and training the community.

147

Child Protective Services Evaluates Cases

An agency known as Child Protective Services (CPS) exists in each of the United States, most often as a division of the state or county welfare department. CPS makes decisions about preventing and intervening in cases of abuse and neglect. The agency provides a variety of services to families and victims, speaking to the needs of particular individuals.

The process of helping the troubled family begins with identification of the problem. The agency charged with locating abusive or neglectful families begins by identifying and reporting the situation. If the agency is alerted from an outside source, the report must be verified. The facts are checked and double checked, sometimes with a slowness that seems unbearable to the concerned neighbor who reported the abuser. However, once the abuse or neglect has been documented, investigation begins.

CPS is customarily responsible for assessing the situation. When the case is confirmed, the agency then plans how it can best help the children and other family members. The best available treatment is determined, considering what's practical and possible. Referrals are made wherever possible.

The family is given the opportunity, sometimes under threat of court order, to heal. Recovery may be presented as an alternative. Adults and children receive therapy, protection, or support.

Before CPS closes the books on a case, a follow-up procedure is required. Every step of the process is coordinated through the central agency, using any available resources or support systems. Legal and administrative requirements must have been met and verified. The ways chosen for dealing with the family's issues are reported. Treatment and referrals are documented. Even the closing of a case and the follow-up investigation must be recorded. This is done for every reported case, regardless of the outcome.

The System Works Slowly

Those who suspect child or adolescent abuse or neglect may be frustrated with the cumbersome investigation system. A report made in error can seriously harm an innocent person's life, yet a youngster left unprotected and exposed to abuse or neglect can be destroyed. It is a heavy balance.

When a juvenile's welfare is clearly in immediate danger, law enforcement officials must respond. It is their legal responsibility, although their methods may vary. Some may simply report the situation to the judicial system and wait for the court to do the rest. Others may act first, arresting the offending adults or taking custody of abused youths. Each agency uses different methods of dealing with reported abuse within its jurisdiction.

The court welfare system is usually responsible for deciding what's best for the child or adolescent. This is true when the juvenile is the offender, and also when the

149

youngster is the victim. The parents' rights also must be respected, especially since many of these cases are not clear-cut. Adults may hire an attorney to defend them before a judge.

Some communities offer what is known as a guardian *ad litem* program. Under this plan a volunteer adult takes an advocacy position for the child or children involved. The advocate is unconcerned with anything except the best interests of the youngsters. The advocate becomes intimately involved with the court process, speaking for the child and calling the judge's attention to special circumstances.

Other communities have a family court system that specializes in domestic law. A particular judge or judges are chosen to deal primarily with these issues. The theory behind this suggests that when there is educated continuity in the position of the decision maker, repeat cases aren't so easily overlooked. Major issues become familiar scenarios if the judge sees related dysfunctional patterns emerging in family after family. The judge also gets to know repeat offenders, making it more difficult for abusers or irresponsible parents to escape treatment or justice through excuses or other maneuvers. Individuals who make return trips to court develop their own reputation and the judge recognizes them.

Whatever the setup of the justice system in a particular community, the courts are charged with representing the best interests of the child. It is up to the judge to decide if a youngster should be removed from the home or left to cope with the family situation. It is up to the judge to decide what agencies must get involved or what parents are required to do.

Many Reports Come From Helping Professionals

Frequently cases of abuse are referred to the court system by health-care professionals. Physicians and nurses are required by law to report cases they suspect are victims of abuse or neglect. This may be one reason why medical personnel are often key figures in diagnosis and reporting. They are often the first to see an injury. They have the expertise to tell if an injury was truly accidental or if it might have been intentionally caused. They are aware of the nature and extent of the injury, so they can better judge how it occurred.

According to Dr. George Commerci, a physician who deals with these situations, "The prime responsibility of the health professional who confronts a case of suspected abuse is to care for the child. Once the immediate medical needs have been met, the appropriate authorities will enter the case. They, and not the doctor, will conduct the investigation. The doctor can contribute by determining whether the child's caretakers have supplied an adequate explanation for the trauma."

School personnel are another source of reports of child abuse and neglect. These individuals see the youngsters daily, getting to know their attitudes and their behavior. They should play a major role in identifying troubled families.

151

While potentially a major reporting source, school personnel are now responsible for only a small percentage of the actual reported cases of child abuse or neglect. There are various reasons that may explain this trend.

School employees or volunteers should be the first to spot and report an abused or neglected child, but they're usually not. For one thing, it is easy to buy into the role of protector or enabler for an abusive family. The thought that one reported incident could cause a child to be separated from parents, even parents who don't know how to treat their families right, is a scary idea. Teachers who come to know and love a particular student may start to see the problem through the child's eyes. They want to maintain the family at all costs. They want to see things get better, so they believe they will. They see the child improve, or have a good week, so they wait for change. They are hopeful or sympathetic rather than realistic and responsible. It's an easy mistake to make. No one, even when abuse is suspected, wants to be the home-wrecker.

Another factor that may hold back reports from teachers and other school personnel may be the danger to the adult who identifies the family. If the suspected abuse is denied and not verified, the parents file slander or punitive lawsuits against the person who pointed the finger. A truly violent individual may confront the accuser directly, if the person's identity is known. Many agencies allow for anonymous reporting, but there may be only one person in a position to know about the abuse. Some investigators may require the name of the person making the report so that they can return for firsthand information during investigation. Sometimes, the reporter may be the only one who can testify that abuse occurred and the person may be called into court.

School Systems Have Power to Effect Change

There are other ways the school system can effect change for dysfunctional families. Schools often serve communities in many ways besides meeting public education requirements. They are meeting places, the focus of social networks, and rallying points for sports events. Most families, even isolated ones, are used to activities and events that take place at schools.

This familiarity with the school facilities and resources provides an excellent opportunity for the educational system to support the needs of families. They regularly distribute information through flyers, newsletters, notes home, and by word-of-mouth. Parenting classes can give needy and healthy families a forum for learning parenting skills and building a support network. Guest speakers or workshops can tackle current issues such as sex education and AIDS or building self-esteem in children. Rooms can be made available for self-help and support groups for parents and children. Some district schools already offer classes to both adolescents and adults on parenting or leadership skills and effective conflict resolution.

A variety of other service agencies may be available in some communities. These range from welfare, counseling centers, and crisis intervention teams to shelters for victims and telephone hot lines. All are attempts to strengthen the family—some emotionally, some financially.

153

Self-Help Groups Can Help Parents Change

Parents who are aware they have problems may be willing to participate in self-help programs such as Parents Anonymous (PA), Parents United, Alcoholics Anonymous (AA), Adult Children of Alcoholics, or Codependents Anonymous. Frequently based on a positive affirmation program such as the Twelve Steps of AA, these support groups are voluntary and funded by donation. They encourage participants to explore their pasts, their issues with compulsive behavior or addictions, and the ways they are changing for the better.

Parents Anonymous specifically targets the needs of abusive or neglectful families. The organization has particular interest in reaching the potential abuser before violence or damage occurs.

The self-help process is designed to interrupt the cycle of abuse through several steps. First, a camaraderie develops among participants so that the parents' feelings of isolation are relieved. They have a safe place to turn with their problems and issues.

Like other support groups, PA gives the participants a forum within which they can develop friends. It is a learning relationship, where parents learn new ways of coping, effective methods of discipline, and loving approaches to child rearing by listening to the other participants.

Attempts at self-improvement are highly applauded, increasing the parents' feelings of self-worth. As the adults begin to feel better about themselves, they begin to trust their decisions and develop more empathy with their children.

Finally, participants work to build trust within the group and between members and facilitators. It is this ability to trust each other that frees parents to open up and find a positive outlet for their feelings and frustrations. They learn they are not alone in their experiences of powerlessness, fear, and love with their children.

Social Services Favor Young Children

Some communities have established domestic violence shelters, and rape crisis or women's centers that provide support to victims and children of abusive families. Many provide overnight or short-term care and living space for these individuals. Vocational training, support groups, counseling, and other services also may be available on-site or through related agencies.

When dealing with adolescents and their parents, one issue appears repeatedly. Present efforts to help abusive or neglectful families focus almost exclusively on younger children. Teenagers are often pushed aside in favor of providing aid to families with little ones. Part of the reason is that society views youths as able to defend and take care of themselves. Many people who work in organizations that provide these services feel adolescents can turn to their own support networks outside the home. The result is that teenagers are passed by in the belief they can wait for help.

155

Because teenagers are closer to adulthood and independence, they should be given a higher priority within social services. Youth cases are now often given second place because professionals expect the young people to have access to help outside the family. The problem with this attitude is that it does not consider that abused teenagers have probably faced maltreatment throughout their lives. They may have reached the age and size of adolescence, but they most likely have very little knowledge about what is available or possible. They have been as isolated as their parents and probably have fewer social skills, so outreach is never even considered by the youths. When it is, the chances are that most available programs won't be designed to handle or help teenagers.

Service Agencies Need to Combine Efforts

More coordination is needed between protective services and the youth service networks. Case planning, program development, and implementation of all need to be interwoven. This would be encouraged if a special position were created for an adolescent worker. That person would work specifically with teens, developing continuity and ties between youth services and protective agencies.

A particular need exists for short- and long-term placements suitable for teenagers. Usually the abused or neglected youth who are placed outside the home have to go into institutions instead of healthy foster homes. Young people may be rejected from private family placements because they have been unmanageable, rejected by their parents, or because they have psychological damage resulting from their painful upbringing. The answer is for community workers to try harder to find alternatives before placing adolescents in institutions. The preferred arrangement would be in a good foster home or in a shelter where they can get the required individual attention.

While they may not have all the answers or the ability to reach out for help, abused or neglected adolescents who come to the attention of agencies need to be heard. They need some say in what happens to them or where they go when removed from their homes. Although teenagers are struggling for their independence, they still need the security of a home. While they try to separate from their family and to gain some control, they need the limits and boundaries a healthy family environment can provide. Youthful victims know what they need and want, so they should be given the opportunity to express them. Moreover, they need to know their preferences will be considered when placement decisions are being made.

When the teenagers' need to find a supportive, home-like environment outside their families is ignored, it is unlikely that youths will seek their own positive resources. Usually adolescents in these cases are used to finding only tension, chaos, or abuse at home, frequently accompanied by feelings of rejection. They have no reason to expect to find support in a different home environment. They are more likely to search for a replacement family outside the home in the form of a negative peer group or gang.

Many other issues need to be considered when trying to help these young people. The coordination of efforts between the juvenile justice system and child protective services needs serious attention. This includes such moves as educational training and informational exchanges between agencies. Educational programs urgently need to address the topics of adolescent development and family dynamics.

Professionals Need to Know More

Education in adolescent issues is vital. Persons working with adolescent abuse cases need to be familiar with the dynamics of abuse—its causes, effects and indicators. An awareness of the particular issues affecting teenagers in these families is imperative. The service provider needs to be able to recognize when some teenage behaviors are masking the real issues or problems. The social worker or agency representative also needs to be aware of the real possibility of abuse and neglect of youths. The only real chance of making a difference occurs when workers can work with the family as a whole, having the skills to intervene in a crisis and to see the true implications of characteristic behaviors.

Any future efforts toward dysfunctional family intervention needs to make the most efficient use possible of the community's resources. Religious organizations, schools, clinics, and help centers can combine their attempts to meet the needs of families where adolescent abuse occurs. Networks of professional services can facilitate working together on cases. A community resource analysis also may be used to plan more integrated service networks for adolescents themselves.

If the problems stemming from adolescent abuse and neglect are to be effectively addressed, future efforts also must include a provision for more personal attention for adolescent victims and their parents. Community support is urgently needed by these families, who are often isolated. The adults have inadequate parenting and coping skills, so even the emotional support provided by self-help groups may not be enough. These parents need to learn:

1. How to communicate with their children or their own parents

2. How to be an effective parent or how to meet the needs of their teenagers

3. How to handle everyday situations and conflicts arising from normal adolescent development

4. How to resolve conflict when it arises

Recovering parents and adolescents may require personal attention to know they are doing "okay." They may need someone to turn to during a crisis they feel they can't handle. Groups offer support, but often it isn't on a personal level. Other times individuals feel their situation is different. They can't relate to what they are learning in the group in terms of their lives and need someone to help them close the gap.

Having Fun Together Helps With Healing

Emotional, financial, or educational support services may still not be enough. Communities need to offer activities and services in which adults and youths can participate together. The distance between parents and teenagers often develops out of the isolation that results from their involvement in activities that send them in different directions. This weakens the parent-child relationship because they don't know or appreciate each other's interests or hobbies.

Intergenerational activities can bring them together by appealing to both young people and adults. Many communities are unaware of this approach to dealing with idle teenagers or have little encouragement to target the problem. Instead, they are busy putting together Little Leagues or senior centers. These are not incompatible efforts when attention is given to the concerns of other ages, particularly those of adolescents and their parents.

The difference between living embedded in problems and moving into a healthy community lifestyle is believing it is possible and then doing it. The traditional values of a patriarchal society fail to teach us that extensive change is possible, that we can make choices and take actions that come from knowing what feels right. But there are those who are finding alternatives, who are constructing new social orders where each person's needs, regardless of age, color, economic status, physical ability, affectional orientation, gender, ethnic heritage or religious beliefs are fulfilled.

One example of a community that actively works to speak to the needs of its members is *The Farm*, an intentional living cooperative in Summerville, Tennessee. It began in the 1970s when a group of people with spiritual affinity assembled on a large piece of land, originally living communally and counting approximately 2,000 families as members. Today's economics has altered their lifestyle somewhat, causing a change in philosophy from collective living to a community with single family homes in a cooperative arrangement. Their numbers dropped to half what they had been, as people were forced to leave to find paying work in more metropolitan areas of the country. The spirit of community remains the same, however.

Having an on-site school for the residents' own children has always been a part of *The Farm*, but now there are additional adolescents who live with Farm families so they can attend the cooperative's high school. Some teenagers choose to go to the local public schools, but the alternative is still very popular among the youngsters themselves.

Integrating teenagers into *The Farm* community doesn't stop with school, however. Once primarily a farming collective, now there wouldn't be horses on *The Farm* if the youths didn't take responsibility for them. Many of these young people were reaching adolescence at the same time the community was changing hats. Their parents had to go into nearby towns for jobs and they suddenly had to begin paying tuition to attend the collective school. The work of running the homestead still had to be done, though most of the adult residents had less time to devote to the community. These circumstances forced the teenagers to take an active role in providing the funds they needed to stay in the school they loved, and to keep the cooperative going.

Now, the young people have a lot to say about what their curriculum includes and about how they choose to live their lives on *The Farm*. They still stay in single family dwellings with their parents or a host family. They still go to school and have chores. They still revel and they still go through the same developmental stages as other teenagers. The difference at *The Farm* is that age doesn't determine the worth of a person nor the expectations the community has for them. Teenagers are actively involved in keeping the cooperative alive. Parents must be actively involved in their children's lives because they are intimately involved with the running of the community and the school. It is an intricate web of community, family, and a microcosm of society that has thus far withstood the tests of time.

Summary

No member of our society can avoid the impact of abusive and neglectful families. Adolescents who are the victims of these dysfunctional families need more than an isolated, one-shot intervention. They need a full-fledged community effort to deal with the effects of maltreatment and the social problems behind it. Social service and law enforcement agencies are already working on the problem with the judicial system, but they are often forced to work on overloaded case schedules with archaic support systems.

Successful communities combine the efforts of these institutions with schools, self-help programs, family shelters, support networks and organized recreational activities.

They speak to the financial, social, emotional, educational, spiritual and physical needs of abused and neglected adolescents and their families. There is potential for great social change toward wholeness when professionals, neighbors, governmental leaders and dysfunctional family survivors unite to create a positive future.

10

Prevention
Act, Don't React

Some old sayings have merit. Some "old wives" knew what they were talking about when they told tales.

A bird in the hand is worth two in the bush.

Don't count your chickens before they hatch.

An ounce of prevention is worth a pound of cure.

The scars of an abusive or neglectful childhood can never be erased. Recovery is a long, involved process that requires active participation and dedication by those who wish to heal. Sometimes nothing helps at all.

Emphasis in the health field is leaning more and more toward prevention. Primary prevention means taking measures to assure that a problem does not occur in the first place. There are diets for a healthy heart, exercises to

165

strengthen the back, vitamins and minerals to maintain healthy blood. Even cancer seems avoidable when proper care is taken to reduce risk factors. Health food stores flourish. Staying healthy isn't just a California trend anymore.

Prevention is also possible for society's ills, including cases of abuse and neglect. Adolescent abuse can be stopped before it occurs, but only if primary prevention is used to modify the behaviors of potentially abusive or neglectful individuals. These people can be helped by teaching them appropriate behaviors and coping strategies through such vehicles as parent training programs and stress management education.

Primary Prevention

When dealing with social problems such as adolescent abuse, primary prevention begins with strengthening an at-risk population. This is done to help people resist violence or neglect, work through their issues, and neutralize the conditions that cause the problems.

Total elimination of adolescent abuse and neglect would take more than a lifetime. It would be unrealistic to try. Still, problems such as stress, inadequate parenting skills, financial limitations, and insufficient health care can be targeted.

When parents are in the midst of struggle, it is nearly impossible for them to focus on one problem at a time. Complications seem overwhelming. Each child, regardless of how badly wanted, presents more needs that must be filled, more responsibilities that must be handled. A delicate balance is required simply to get through the day.

With help from community resources, parents and victims alike can learn how to better handle the stresses of their particular situation. When dysfunctional family members join with others in classes or programs that teach conflict resolution, parenting skills, or stress management, they learn methods that work. They learn new ways to try to deal with daily life and effective substitutes for bad habits. At the same time, they can learn by modeling the way healthy families cope and interact.

Parents Under Stress Are Most At Risk

Parents who are ill but must keep going anyway are likely candidates for abuse or neglect. They feel bad, yet they have no alternative. Public health-care screenings and clinics can make the difference for people who cannot afford the rising costs of medical care or insurance. Sometimes just having access to medicine makes all the difference.

Financial pressure may be the greatest problem. It's very difficult to feel self-esteem when making choices between weekly groceries and a warm winter coat. No matter how great the desire to take care of the family, no matter how loving the parents, making these kinds of choices hurts everyone. Agencies that provide food, services and other forms of financial assistance speak to the needs of the less fortunate and give poorer families a decent chance in life.

167

Unfortunately, even giving money to these economically disadvantaged families does not erase the classism of today's society. The clothes one wears, the way one speaks, and the cultural exposure one has, greatly determines where one is accepted. The poor and homeless, despite recent national altruistic efforts, are generally despised and scorned. They are blamed for their condition. The fact that most of these people started out with far fewer advantages than those who look down on them carries little weight in society in general.

Classism shows up in parenting classes that are offered without free child care. Working-class and poor families are discriminated against when the nearest available resources are located far from their neighborhoods—in places that require automobile transportation and money for gas. These are limitations that middle- and upper-class professionals forget when trying to help. These issues can only be changed when those in power, those who don't need the services, begin to question their classist attitudes. Not thinking about these needs is just as discriminatory as fighting against helping the less advantaged.

Of course, even when successful efforts are made in the primary prevention of abuse and neglect, the problems aren't completely solved. Prevention efforts may not eliminate the issues that cause maltreatment, but they do help reduce the frequency with which this occurs.

Secondary Prevention Introduces Treatment

Secondary prevention involves the early identification and treatment of a problem. The purpose here is to minimize the duration of abuse or neglect, focusing on stopping its recurrence. Accomplishing this usually requires treating developmental issues of both the parents and the children. Puberty and mid-life crises must be addressed, giving both adults and teenagers a supportive forum in which to air their problems. Opening communication among generations helps promote understanding.

Another important secondary prevention measure is teaching conflict resolution. Parents who don't know how to talk about their problems or how to negotiate compromises can't very well teach these skills to their children. They are likely to act too permissive, which becomes neglectful, or to rely on power, which turns to abuse. They may feel they have to either direct the family or give up entirely. When they learn new ways to deal with issues in their lives, they find themselves better able to deal with their children.

It is important at this stage to reduce the family's isolation. When adults enroll in and attend parenting classes or other training, they are forced into interactions with others. They make friends in a healthy environment and ideally are influenced by their mutual attempts at self-improvement. They also learn more about community resources and places they can turn for help when it's needed.

These steps also encourage improved communication skills. Simply by talking and interacting more with others, these parents learn about communication. They build those skills further as they share in classes and when they meet with those who can help them.

All the secondary measures may stop the abuse or neglect before it goes any further. Parents who find resources and learn skills to improve their lives may respond simply because someone has shown an interest in them. When the interest is directed in helpful ways, the course of their futures can be changed for the better. They can change when they see the world around them changing, becoming more friendly and supportive.

Since this is an imperfect world, many cases of adolescent abuse or neglect will not come to light until the situation is already underway. Primary and secondary prevention may be too late to be effective, but at that point it is still possible to use tertiary prevention.

Tertiary Prevention - A Last Resort

The third step, tertiary prevention, involves efforts to keep the problem from getting worse. It also involves rehabilitating the client. While primary prevention takes place before the abuse or neglect occurs, both secondary and tertiary efforts are made when the negative patterns have already begun. It is always preferable to use prevention before any damage is done. The earlier the cycle of abuse and neglect is interrupted, the easier it is to stop the negative behavior.

This is the type of help that adolescents receive when their dysfunction reaches the point that residential care is necessary. Usually the problems have become so overwhelming for the teenagers that some extraordinary measure has been taken. There may have been criminal delinquency, a suicide attempt, an uncontrollable outbreak of violence or emotional breakdown that results in finally getting the youngsters the direct attention needed. When this help comes as hospitalization and rehabilitation, a team of health care professionals may be involved. This approach allows for medical, psychological, educational, and other specialists to work with the young people in a protected environment, but it also occurs after other methods have been attempted and failed to help them.

Indeed, prevention can take many forms. One obvious way to encourage healthy behavior is to increase the public's knowledge of the problems of adolescent abuse and neglect. Sometimes people simply aren't aware of what sort of treatment constitutes abuse or neglect. They don't realize the deep effects of capital punishment, or that the misuse of power over young people can discolor their entire adulthoods. By educating the general population we begin to create an understanding of both the problem and its repercussions.

Subsidized Quality Child Care Can Help

Increasing the availability and affordability of child care in society is another way of encouraging healthy parenting. Corporate sponsored or government subsidized day-care programs give parents the opportunity to earn a decent living without constant worry. Although many communities in the United States operate Head Start programs for the economically disadvantaged, these preschools reach only a minority of those who desperately need them.

The first, most obvious, advantage of financially sponsored quality child-care is that the parents are relieved of worry and stress simply by knowing their youngsters are in a healthy, safe environment during the working day. Sometimes the working hours are the only time single or overburdened parents have to themselves. The workplace can be a source of strength to potential abusers because, in a positive environment, they gain self-esteem and the ability to see themselves outside a responsible, parental role.

Today nearly 50 percent of U.S. mothers with children younger than one work outside the home. Congress has addressed this issue through the introduction of the ABC Child Care Bill and subsequent similar measures, attempting to fund and legislatively encourage increased accessibility to affordable, quality day-care.

Perhaps the most cost-effective and earliest preventive measure that can be taken to help at-risk children is quality preschool. A cost-benefit analysis of a preschool program and its results showed that investment in a one-year preschool program provided a return of seven times the cost, based on an analysis of program costs, learning abilities, and the degree to which those studied used social services. However, there are long-reaching implications of addressing child-care issues, effects that extend into the adolescent years.

A longitudinal study begun more than 30 years ago with economically disadvantaged families shows the long-range impact of early intervention through preschool education. The study followed participants into adulthood and discovered they "began to experience and demonstrate greater success in school, greater commitment to schooling, higher school achievement and reinforcement of a more success oriented role by teachers, parents and peers."

This project led to the funding of Head Start, but the study has continued to show positive effects. At end of the first year, researchers found that the children's IQs had raised twenty-seven points. Eventually, after children got to school, they were less likely to be held back a grade, stayed in school longer, earned better grades, and had better attendance. This carried over into high school, where these students had a lower dropout rate and were more likely to hold after-school jobs and to graduate. More of these young people went on to college.

Preschoolers Make Successful Adults

Recent findings have gone on to indicate that those children who participated in the most open-ended preschool program have been the most successful as adults. In contrast, children who were involved in a highly structured, academic curriculum as preschoolers had more social problems than the others. They had more problems, with the law and within their families, than those who attended either a traditional preschool program or an open-ended approach using child-directed learning centers. Most successful at preventing later problems in life was the Hi

Scope approach, where children were offered a selection of activities and encouraged to make choices about what to do.

This further supports the position that when people, even children, are given some control over their lives, they are less likely to resort to acting out their frustrations in abusive or neglectful behaviors. Beginning this approach in the preschool years is one of the most direct forms of primary prevention.

Providing support systems is also important for all three levels of prevention. Child care and after-school or latchkey programs for older children and adolescents are important links, especially at the middle school or junior high age. However, there are other ways to offer support for parents and youngsters.

Spiritual organizations have traditionally offered youth and family programs that meet these needs, although overzealous religious sects may do more harm than good when they encourage hard-line dogma. Again, restrictions that take decision-making power away from individuals of any age foster resentment and acting out of anger and negative emotions.

Social service agencies present support systems in the form of counselors, therapy groups, financial aid, and more traditional programs.

Self-Help Offers Positive Alternative

A newer network of support for dysfunctional families is emerging from the field of addiction and recovery. Self-help groups ask only for voluntary donations, making them more accessible to those who are above the poverty level but cannot afford or don't believe in conventional therapy.

These groups may represent one of the strongest steps toward changing values and beliefs about family violence. Other forms of public relations contribute to perhaps the most widely used technique for increasing social awareness of the problems of abuse and neglect.

Heightened public awareness can be achieved through mass media coverage. Newspapers and magazines increasingly focus on family issues as more and more individuals become willing to tell their stories. Television and radio talk shows, news reports of arrests and convictions in child abuse cases, movies that address these issues, and other forms of media outreach help people develop empathy. Sometimes just hearing about others who have experienced abuse or neglect may alert parents or young people to their own personal issues. Those who grew up in dysfunctional, abusive, or neglectful families may realize the truth about their lives for the first time thanks to this kind of outreach.

Training programs, workshops, and classes that teach about healthy behavior as well as about abuse and neglect are effective vehicles for raising public consciousness. Individuals must know the causes, indicators, and effects of adolescent maltreatment if they are to recognize its impact on society and their own lives. People need to know the procedures for reporting adolescent abuse or neglect and where to find the resources to help the family heal.

A desirable effect of so much publicity and awareness of the problems is that as people know more, the likelihood of abuse or neglect occurring is decreased. Education is half the battle.

People Need to Learn About Alternatives

Interestingly, places of education may be the most effective source of outreach and consciousness raising. Six themes concerning the role of schools in the problem of child maltreatment are stressed in current literature:

1. Because schools are concerned with the whole child, seeking help for the youth in trouble is compatible with educational objectives.

2. Educators and others who work directly with children have an excellent opportunity and a grave responsibility to identify and properly report suspected cases of child abuse and neglect.

3. Education in the United States is potentially a major source for helping children and their families, but this potential has rarely been tapped.

4. Although educators are generally mandated to report suspected abuse or neglect, the requirement is widely disregarded. There are seldom clear-cut channels for

reporting. The extent of the school's involvement is uncertain. At the same time, few professionals are more genuinely concerned about children than teachers.

5. The school system must be convinced, pressured, lobbied, or even coerced to initiate parenting skills and childhood development courses for every pre-school, elementary, and junior and senior high school student.

6. The school utilizing paddling or corporal punishment is a place where the only legally and socially sanctioned abuse of children exists. It is an endorsement of violence by the institution that, after the family, is the most important socializing agent in the United States.

The fact that society sees schools in these roles makes it very possible for educators to be a strong source of support for maltreated adolescents and their families. The reality is that few take the initiative to do so.

Some teachers may feel hindered by a lack of knowledge about abuse and neglect. They may question their perceptions of the problem, particularly in the case of adolescents who are actively covering up for their parents or hiding their own shame. Educators may feel unclear about how to report suspected cases and what policies cover their actions. They may feel unsupported, fearing sole liability for their actions should they be incorrect in their evaluation of the situation.

Understandably, educators may hesitate to report suspected cases because they believe their efforts will be of little value in the long run. An overload of cases may cause a social worker to dismiss a difficult-to-prove situation or a report that seems less urgent than others. Intervention may be temporary and result in the youngster being returned to the same situation after a brief interlude during which the student's own schooling may be disrupted. When this sort of thing happens several times, teachers tend to give what support they can to the youths rather than reporting their families to authorities or agencies.

Schools Have Great Potential to Effect Change

This is the present situation, but it need not be permanent. The U.S.'s school system has great potential to overcome these obstacles and become a primary force in the efforts against abuse and neglect.

Moving in this direction means schools must develop several roles. They must become a support system involved in community education and child advocacy. Educators must become knowledgeable about the dynamics of abuse and neglect, enabling them to become a major reporting source of suspected cases.

In truth, the first role of the school may be that of a support system. It has been said that "schools have a legal, moral and historical mandate to ensure that each and every child has a direct and enduring relationship with adults or groups of adults that have an interest in the child's welfare."

Teachers see the same children every day and often develop close relationships with them. This is true even in the upper grades, when a favorite instructor, club advisor, or coach may become confidant and friend. This gives the educator an excellent opportunity to observe any changes in the child's behavior or demeanor that would suggest possible problems at home. They can compare present and past behavior and appearance, noticing both physical abuse and emotional distress evidenced by decreased grooming or self-care.

From this advantageous position, teachers can clearly observe signs of mistreatment—low self-esteem, anxiety, fearfulness, or extremes in shyness or aggression. When teachers are educated about the signs for which they need to be looking, they will be in key positions for reporting abuse or neglect to the proper authorities.

Others on school staffs can have a vital role in this effort. Lunchroom workers, janitorial staff, teacher aides, and school bus drivers may have more opportunity than teachers to overhear telltale conversations among students. Nonprofessional personnel may be considered more on-par with the youngsters since their home life may be more economically equal to that of at-risk families and because they interact with children from a less authoritative level. When these individuals are taught about the issues and signs of abuse and neglect, they, too, can become an irreplaceable source of help.

Of course, it cannot be assumed that those of lower economic status are the only ones who abuse or neglect their youngsters. Teachers themselves may be as guilty of these behaviors as the parents of their troubled students. While statistics may show that people who have obtained higher educational levels are less likely to fall into the at-risk categories, this does not mean other factors do not enter. The point here is that everyone on the school staff can become child advocates, and that everyone from parent volunteer to secretary to school crossing guard to principal needs to know about these issues. Everyone who sees or interacts with young people is a potential force for change.

Mental Health Professionals Can Open Doors

Counselors or school psychologists can take an even more active role in the prevention and treatment of abuse and neglect. They have a prime opportunity to conduct classes on child rearing, child development and parenting skills. These forums can teach parents about misperceptions of children, youth, and adults while showing them healthier and more effective ways of relating to and communicating with their youngsters and each other.

Teachers and other staff members can join in this process as instructors, leaders, or participants. They, too, need to understand human development. Because most people come from dysfunctional families, almost everyone can benefit from learning about what is the usually expected behavior for individuals of different age groups. When conflict resolution skills are introduced as part of this learning process, the package becomes even more successful.

Currently, many teachers or school personnel hesitate to get involved with families in crisis because they know little about identifying and verifying child abuse. When they lack knowledge, they can't intervene effectively anyway. That's why it's necessary to increase the awareness level of educators and school staffs. Experience has proved that teachers who participated in a teacher-training workshop "began to view child abuse as a community problem and became more willing as community members to take action to alleviate the problem."

Specifically, it was found that this training gave the teachers more knowledge about abuse and more empathy for abusive parents. They were more likely to initiate or support class discussion about potential abuse and less likely to use physical discipline in the classroom. These classes also sparked more conversations and discussions about abuse with friends and colleagues.

Summary

The best way to treat adolescent abuse is to prevent it—by teaching parents how healthy families interact and how they can more successfully communicate with their children. Prevention can happen through community support and with social service programs that give adults an outlet when their lives overwhelm them. But financial and bread-and-butter daily needs such as day-care, medical services and housing also must be addressed.

Similar methods work to change the abusive or neglectful family, encouraging improved communication skills, offering concrete help for real daily problems and providing a support system for families in recovery. The school system offers one of the most accessible vehicles for such prevention, although it is currently underused in most communities. Of course, these mechanisms will only work when those in positions to make the outreach—teachers, counselors, others in helping professions—are willing to make a serious commitment.

11

What Can I Do?
Creating Change

In a small coastal Florida town in an average middle-class public high school there was once a journalism teacher named Joe Berta Bullock. She was known for demanding the most from her students, for ruling the school with an iron fist, and for producing the best student newspapers and yearbooks in the state.

Joe Berta Bullock was differently abled. She stood less than five feet tall with braces and crutches, yet she applied to her teaching the determination with which she fought her physical limitations. One year she was singled out by the President of the United States as a national role model for the handicapped. After her retirement, the county named a school in her honor.

Her former students run major national newspapers, publish novels and nonfiction books, run for office, and defend cases in court. She expected them to demand the most of themselves and to settle for nothing less. She was a teacher who, once encountered, was seldom forgotten.

After having her as their teacher, students' lives were changed. Whether they admired or hated her, her students would never again doubt the ability of a physically challenged individual. And they knew what it felt like never to give up.

Not everyone has the opportunity to learn from such a dynamic figure, but most people have a favorite role model who in some way shaped their past. Teachers, coaches, and other adults working directly with children and teenagers have a tremendous opportunity to influence them. They are in an undisputed position to encourage the development of violence-free family interaction. Teachers can change the world or at least, start the process.

Step One: Identify the Problem

One of the first steps toward helping make change happen is to identify the problem. This is begun by recognizing, confirming and reporting suspected abuse or neglect. Those who do this must have a clear understanding of the legal requirements of their state.

Educators need to be well informed and knowledgeable before entering a case of abuse or neglect. There are three important things to remember when considering filing a report. The rules of most states will be met by following these guidelines.

First, when children's behavior or physical well-being indicates that they are in peril, risk, harm, or jeopardy, a report should be made with a request for further investigation. Second, the established policy for the school district should be followed rather than going it alone. It is important to have backup support. Third, when in doubt, the issue should be resolved in favor of the child's needs.

Important safeguards include verifying the reporting laws of the particular state, the school's reporting policy and procedure, if any, and the school's relationship with the protective agency designated to accept the reports.

If there are several individuals who can make the report together, they should gather certain information about the adolescents and their families. The protective agency will want to know the names of those involved, the victims' names and addresses and reasons for the suspicion. Other problems such as drug abuse, incorrigibility, or pregnancy should be mentioned.

Report All Relevant Information

Background information also should be included about previous abuse, family conflict, drug use, or alcohol problems. Physical or behavioral observations should be documented. Secondary information from school or medical records also may be needed. All these things go into the written collateral that will usually be required following an oral report.

This is not an easy task. Even the best teachers may fail to come up with enough documentation to back up a report, regardless of how sure they are of the abuse or neglect. This is why professionals, including educators and counselors, are often reluctant to report suspected cases. They fear that intervention would be minimal or the case would be rejected. They feel reporting would be a breach of confidential and trusting relationships, particularly for counselors, and that it might hurt their professional reputation.

Other times those who could report adolescent maltreatment believe that it would only worsen the family conflict. They assess the case as not involving a substantial risk for their clients. They assume the juvenile court approach to adolescent abuse and neglect to be ineffective. They may believe there is insufficient evidence to prove allegations in court.

One way to handle this reluctance within the school system is by designating one or several staff members as the persons responsible for reporting abuse and neglect cases. Under this plan, those appointed review proposed reports, assist other agencies in investigating further, and work with victims. These staff members also may take charge of initiating training, counseling, or support groups, working with school personnel to increase their awareness of the problems, and encouraging others to report cases. Officially designating a particular individual as responsible for making reports also may relieve some pressure while providing support for doing so.

Handle Each Case With Care

While silence will not solve the problem, it is vital that teachers and other school personnel don't become involved in cases in ways that make matters worse for the victims, the parents, or themselves. It is natural to feel anger, repulsion, disgust, and other negative emotions toward the parents or even toward a delinquent juvenile despite the abuse. However, when approaching the situation from the perspective of an outside authority figure, those involved must be objective. They must put their anger and indignation aside in favor of the victims' best interests.

One of the first events that will occur following a report, or even before the report, is the parent conference. Parents and youths need to be made as comfortable as possible in discussions and interviews dealing with possible abuse. Those introducing the subject to the family need to be empathetic to avoid repercussion if the parents or children become defensive. No good can be done, no change can be made if the family members feel they cannot be honest and open with those expressing concern about their situation.

Parents whose home life includes violence, abuse, or neglect are very likely to feel ashamed or guilty when confronted with reality. Even if one parent is a battered spouse, she or he may resent being discovered or be embarrassed about staying in the relationship. They may fear legal repercussions or worry that they will lose their children, disrupting their family even more. They may be angry at the attempted intervention, seeing their home as private territory and resenting any attempts to alter it from outside.

187

Guidelines for Dealing With Families

The following eight guidelines may be helpful when preparing to face family members:

1. *Establish rapport with parents and teenagers.* Begin with casual conversation about community events, school sports competitions, or common interests. It might help to begin by commenting on something positive in which the youths are involved or by complementing the youngsters on some recent progress. Wait for the family to relax slightly as they get to know the staff.

2. *Listen to both feelings and words.* The *way* something is said may indicate more than the actual words. Staff members involved in these conferences are likely to have a good idea about what is going on, so they will sense clues about what's really happening. It is important to trust this perception.

3. *Encourage the parents to clarify their feelings.* Many people in this position will not readily use feeling words such as happy, sad, angry, anxious, glad. They will be more likely to tell what they think is the case or to give their analysis of the situation. Keep on target, even if it means repeating the question many different ways until feelings emerge.

4. *Keep the conference on task.* Getting bogged down in the details of a specific incident or letting the parent go on with complaints about the youths will serve no one. This is the time to uncover the suspected abuse or neglect.

5. *Show empathy for the parents and children*. Staff members who nod and make notes appear insensitive and unconcerned. Checking a watch for the time or answering phone calls during conversation only hurt the process and make those involved feel inconsequential. It is important to give the family a chance to express their feelings without judgment. Active listening skills are vital, confirming that the speaker's feelings are being communicated and that the listener understands.

6. *Communicate feelings of open trust and confidentiality*. Never reveal the identities or specifics of another family. Listen openly, avoiding judgment about language use, mode of dress, economic or religious values, or lifestyles. When these families are revealing their private lives, they must trust the outsider or they will never speak honestly. If the staff member is unable to merit this trust, then another person should be appointed to handle the conference. When parents or teenagers feel threatened, they will be uncooperative and even more secretive.

7. *Recognize your own feelings and nonverbal cues while dealing with the parents*. Staff members who have prejudged a situation or who are so set in their value system that they cannot accept that others have different, equally valid, morals will make ineffective counselors. Ethnic, economic, social, religious, or lifestyle differences are not the issue. This is the time to concentrate on abuse or neglect. Other personal choices are not relevant and should not be judged. The staff person involved should be able to deal

189

objectively with these situations and should be aware of body language that communicates negative emotions such as disapproval, boredom, or rejection.

8. *Assess the point beyond which the parents' cooperation is lost.* This is the fine art of knowing when to stop, of not going too far. Parents who are turned off or feel attacked at the first meeting will be twice as hard to reach the next time. In intervention as in parenting, leadership holds much more influence than force. The goal is to effect change within the family; to improve relationships with as little disruption as possible.

Parents naturally don't want to be condemned for their actions. They may have been abused themselves and know no other way of coping, yet they may not like the way they live. They may already be embarrassed and uncomfortable for being singled out. If they are to cooperate, they must be assured that the staff wants to help and that they want what's best for the children.

Optimal conditions occur when the parents believe they have the same objectives as the staff—looking after the child's best interest. However, it is important to remember that most parents in this situation will feel a need to be in control. If they feel alienated, judged, patronized, or dominated, they are likely to reject any further attempts to help. After that, there are few alternatives. Unless the judicial system steps in, the staff will have to wait and hope for parent-initiated meetings.

Parents Need to Get Involved

Another avenue to helping these dysfunctional families is to encourage parental involvement in the youths' activities or school events. Opening the door to support groups or parenting programs may give the adults the contact with peers that they desperately need, especially if socially or geographically isolated.

Families at risk should be encouraged to get involved in programs that teach useful skills, alleviate stress and frustration, or introduce crisis management. While simple social interaction can be beneficial, these parents need a forum in which to open up and share their concerns or problems. They need a peer group who understands their point of view yet is actively finding new ways to improve.

Parents Anonymous and Parents United are two groups that offer support to families dealing with these issues. Their goal is to improve the parents' self-confidence and encourage healthy family life. Adults who participate openly also learn to share their feelings and fears, identifying with others and learning new ways of dealing with daily pressures.

Workshops and support groups that are offered to dysfunctional families should identify and enhance parental strengths. These self-confidence-building experiences may cover topics ranging from human development, positive discipline, sexuality, building independence, resolving conflict, or understanding feelings. Initial activities should involve easily accomplished goals, providing a sense of achievement and success.

191

Parents who feel they are failing or are disappointed in the early stages of these activities may become discouraged or frustrated and leave the group. This is why early tasks must pinpoint each person's strengths. Once identified, these strengths can begin to overshadow and replace weaknesses in coping with life's problems.

Fact finding, reporting, and providing family support is a beginning. But more effort is needed. There are several other qualitative issues that affect the success of a community's or organization's adolescent abuse prevention efforts.

Communities Must Speak to Needs of Youths

Attempts to prevent adolescent maltreatment need to begin by defusing and controlling family violence. High standards for the care of children and youth should be established and maintained, demonstrating the community's interest in its children and families. Social values and structures that strengthen all sorts of families throughout their life course should be encouraged. Finally, ongoing study should examine the human ecology of the maltreatment of children and youth to improve the reservoir of research-based knowledge.

Society has already begun to move away from endorsing violence. Adults who were subjected to childhood abuse or neglect have started to speak out against such treatment. They are facing their own resulting issues and encouraging a move toward a peaceful, healthy family life.

A first step in this process is creating an ethic of non-violence. A peaceful existence happens in an environment that doesn't approve of violence in any form and that doesn't use violence to solve problems. Now is the time to initiate a climate that will nurture a peace-oriented morality. That means providing an environment that is supportive and that uses positive reinforcement and good leadership rather than corporal punishment as discipline.

Next, we can teach parents nonviolent ways to lead or discipline their children. This is one of the most practical ways to prevent abuse. Corporal punishment easily becomes unintentional abuse. Parents who resort to spanking or more severe forms of physical discipline may hit their children harder or more times than the adult intended or realizes. Anger can cause parents to become overzealous in their attempts at control, making the punishment much worse than the crime deserved.

When youngsters reach adolescence, corporal punishment begins to lose what little effectiveness it may have had when the children were younger. Parents who know no other way of handling their youths increase the physical force on which they rely to control their teenagers' behavior.

There are alternatives. Even adults can learn new methods of parenting that work. Alternative means of discipline and effective leadership techniques can be taught in parenting classes, workshops, and support groups. Both parents and adolescents can learn these skills by participating together and with their peers.

Teens Have Special Needs

Adolescents in this country are believed to have the right to education, health care, clothing, and a balanced diet. These seem like the basics, yet many teenagers don't get this basic care. Their needs differ from those of younger children.

Age and maturity level must be considered when caring for and supervising adolescents. Teenagers may not need as much supervision as younger children, but they still need some guidance. The amount needed depends on the individual. Youths are so different when it comes to maturity that two fifteen-year-olds may need two different levels of supervision and care. One may be just fine when left alone for a day or two while another may be unable to handle that much independence. However, clearly neither should be left alone for long periods of time.

When rearing teenagers, it is important to remember that they are struggling for their independence and have the right to a certain amount of freedom concerning their lives. It is also a time when young people are learning to set their own boundaries and limits. They need to feel secure. They need to know they have a safe environment in which to grow and develop.

Adolescents need to understand the standards of care they should expect. They should be taught that they should be receiving proper health care and nutrition, what that means, and why it's important. They need to be impressed with the value of an education and that they have the right to one. Only when *both* teenagers and their parents understand the care and the supervisory needs of youth can adolescents begin to feel secure.

Adolescents Need Adult Friends

Meaningful interpersonal relationships with responsible, caring adults make the difference between an emotionally healthy adolescent and an unbalanced, needy teenager. These grown-up friends or family members open doors when they talk with adolescents, reacting positively to situations that arise. They enable youths to feel secure, and give them someone to turn to in times of trouble.

Local communities can be made teenager-friendly as well. Adolescents need access to supportive organizations that show both the youth and their families that the community is interested in their welfare and cares what happens to them. Community support can take the form of financial aid, shelter, youth organizations, adult organizations, and medical assistance. These efforts can be aimed directly at teenagers, at their parents, or at whole families.

Financial assistance works best when government and other public funds are directed to pay for professional or volunteer services for those needing help. This is different from simply giving out money. Instead, funding is provided for the specific kinds of help needed. These things include child care, parent education, and child protective services.

The availability of professional mental health and social services signals the community's interest in preventing adolescent abuse. However, many of these professional services need to modify the existing programs, policies, and procedures if they truly want to accommodate to the needs of teenagers. This can only happen when resources are shifted to provide new programs, to tailor existing programs to serve adolescent needs, and to broaden the capacity of services already provided.

Additional community efforts to serve adolescents include hotline, residential care where teenagers can go during crisis periods, and counseling services.

Strengthening the Family Bond

While external support is being increased in the surrounding community, abusive and neglectful families need to learn ways to strengthen their internal structure. A weak family unit leads to maltreatment, while a strong bond among family members increases the psychological and social resources of parents. This is believed also to increase the likelihood that these parents can and will provide adequate care for their children.

Three such efforts to help strengthen families are external support systems, natural helping networks, and self-help groups.

Health-care organizations, schools, clergy and other agencies that can guide families through difficult times provide external support systems for troubled families. They are available throughout various stages of human development and deal with the particular problems of each stage. While these agencies are not there to provide ongoing supervision, they do help resolve problems and crises that parents or adolescents feel they can't handle alone.

Natural helping networks are comprised of relatives, friends, and neighbors upon whom families would naturally call when necessary. Most people do turn to these sources for help when handling day-to-day situations. These mutual support systems need legitimization and encouragement, although they may have the oldest legacy. Everyone needs friends to talk with and rely on in emergencies—big or small. The problem is that abusive parents often isolate themselves from just such support. They trust neither neighbors nor relatives. It takes time and commitment for these people to risk trusting those who could be part of their natural helping network. When they do gain the confidence of the needy, dysfunctional parent, the relationship that develops will be beneficial to both parties.

Self-help groups such as Parents Anonymous and Parents United are usually effective. These supportive organizations work on improving the individual's self-confidence, self-esteem, conflict resolution, crisis management, and interpersonal relationships. This is just the beginning of the changes encouraged by these programs.

All these efforts can be beneficial in many ways. They handle many different types of situations. They cost little to run and work to strengthen the family. This strength is the key to preventing adolescent abuse and neglect.

Young Parents Have Their Own Issues

These measures are doubly necessary when the cause of abuse and neglect is parental immaturity. When a baby is born to teenagers, the odds are that the parents are still children themselves at the time of birth. They probably have not resolved their developmental issues and lack mature parenting skills. This makes them prime candidates to abuse and neglect their infants and adolescents.

Children of teenage mothers, who usually end up with the babies, are more likely to be maltreated, especially through physical neglect. Undoubtedly, there is a need to increase the adolescent mother's educational and social support in order to enable a higher quality of life for both mother and child.

Sex education is another valuable measure that cannot be ignored. Young people need the facts before they experiment. They need to know measures to take to prevent pregnancy. If birth control is not used or fails to work, adolescents need to know the options for handling the situation should pregnancy occur.

Teenagers who decide to complete the pregnancy and keep their babies can still be taught effective parenting skills in order to be adequately prepared for the realities of the situation they are facing. They can be prepared through pre- and post-natal care classes and in instruction on child development. This type of educational support is practical, but also helps ease some of the young expectant parents' fear, frustration and anxiety. When backed up by peer support groups, these programs can help adolescent parents find support among those who understand their feelings in this very difficult time.

Summary

In every person's life are individuals who have great impact. These are the adults who have the great opportunity to help abused adolescents and their families. They are also the ones who face the responsibility of deciding when reports must be made and what interventions in family affairs are necessary for the health and well-being of the children.

Reporting child or adolescent abuse cannot be treated lightly. Much background information must be given. Specific complaints must be documented. Parents must be considered and involved. Open communication is vital.

Self-help and other programs need to be used to teach family members interpersonal skills and to alleviate stress and frustration. Outreach, education and practical support can help mature and youthful parents alike, as these families find the ways and means to heal.

12

Intervention
When to Make the Move

The initial crisis is past. Abuse has happened. Neglect has made its impact. Tears have been shed. Anger has reared and settled.

It is time to intervene, to change the present situation. It is time to develop, within the family, a sense of security and nurturance. It is time to establish a sense of "normalcy" in a safe place where people can grow emotionally and socially.

While the timing is ripe there are many intervention strategies that apply. Health-care services can assist physical healing and restore physical balance. Mental health services can help individuals and families to center emotionally. Educational classes give family members better interpersonal skills or improved access to regular employment. Recreation and other forms of community involvement build a supportive network for the healing family.

Reporting Must Come First

First and most important, however, is the reporting of suspected cases of maltreatment. It is mandatory in most states, although each has its own regulations and policies. Many states grant immunity to those who act in "good faith" and impose penalties for those who fail to report. The reason for this is that help only comes to a troubled family after it has been reported to the agencies that provide services—those who protect.

Reporting begins with the compilation of the appropriate information about the adolescent and the family. Once an oral report has been submitted, a written report is customarily required within a certain time span, often seventy-two hours. Besides describing the nature and extent of any injuries, a written report cites other evident problems such as drug or alcohol use or pregnancy. Family background information and other evidence verifying suspicions of abuse or neglect will be needed. Medical and school records should be included with facts such as the names, ages, and addresses of family members.

One issue concerning current methods of reporting is that most cases are referred based on subjective conclusions about the potential for abuse within the family, for which the professional remains solely responsible. If a teacher, for example, believes there is a potentially dangerous home situation, that individual makes the report based on feelings or suspicion. When the teacher is aware and willing to become involved, everything proceeds according to plan.

The problems appear when one considers the teacher's own perspective. If this is a white Protestant male with an upper-middle-class background and upper-middle-class values, and if he has not examined his own issues in life, then he may be blind to the upper- middle-class Protestant father who talks the teacher's language but forces his daughter into incest. This teacher may report dozens of working-class black families for neglect because there is no one home with the children after school or to fix dinner, yet may fail to realize that a computer game, video screen, massive stereo system, and microwave oven give less nurturing and supervision than a houseful of brothers and sisters.

It's only natural. We see what we're looking for and we're blind to our own shortcomings. It takes considerable personal growth and political consciousness-raising to be able to look past our own value systems or economic advantages in order to realize the possibilities and limitations others face. This is why objectivity requires standards.

There is a need for an objective means of identification of potentially or actively abusive or neglectful families. It should involve standardized methods of assessment and be more beneficial than subjective in its conclusions.

Identifying Risk Factors

Certain factors have been identified that could be used as criteria in determining families at risk of becoming abusive or neglectful. The earlier these are determined, the more likely prevention is possible. However, when intervention becomes necessary these risk factors will be evident. While certain signals may be identified, it must be remembered that the same criteria can be used consistently and effectively only if they are considered alongside the general characteristics of the population with which the family identifies.

Risk factors to be considered can be observed as early as birth but remain relevant even when the child reaches adolescence. These include:

1. Parents who act indifferent, intolerant, or overanxious toward the child

2. An existing history of family violence

3. Socioeconomic problems such as unemployment

4. A child who had a premature birth or low birth weight

5. Parents who were themselves abused or neglected as children

6. A blended family including a step-parent or cohabitee of a parent

7. A single or separated parent

8. A mother who was younger than twenty-one at the time the child was born

9. A history of mental illness, or drug or alcohol addiction

10. A child who as an infant was separated from the mother for greater than twenty-four hours post-delivery

11. An child who is mentally or physically handicapped

12. Children in the family spaced closer than eighteen months

13. A child who was never breast-fed as an infant

While these factors carry different weight and may affect various families differently, they give the reporting professional some guidance from which to judge the situation. They are not to be taken as the only criteria, but simply as signals.

Background influences and situational stress factors are important. But many forces come into play in the lives of the individuals, the families, the community, and the culture in which these people live. What needs to be seen is not so much the number of risky elements but how the family members interact and cope with their situation.

Taking Action Requires Responsible Commitment

Being in a position of legally or morally having to report an abusive or neglectful family is a tremendous responsibility. It cannot be taken lightly and it cannot be ignored.

205

When you suspect abuse or neglect yet feel you need more information for evidence, keep accurate records of the dates of problems, the extent of any injuries you notice, and any extreme changes in behavior. If you can have direct contact with both parents and their youngsters, note their behavior and interactions as well. Record your impression of the way they treat the teenager, the way the youth responds, and the attitudes they express toward each other. Be clear about the difference between objective reporting of what happened and your opinions of rationale, attitude, the particular family's values or lifestyle, and other subjective issues.

Eventually you will have to turn this report in, so you will need to make a copy for yourself. Remember, this file is confidential. The trust factor with the family is vital, but there also may be legal or social ramifications of any potentially damaging information.

Once you file the report, allow the agency to decide if immediate action should be taken. Your job is to inform, not to solve the problem. You've been observing the situation for some time, but the agency only just received the report. Expect it to take anywhere from a day to a week to reach a decision, depending on the number of active cases the agency has.

Things to Consider Before Filing Charges

If you feel you need to file a formal charge or report of suspected abuse, you are facing an even more difficult decision. It may help to consider the following questions before taking the final steps.

First, what concrete evidence do you have to support your suspicion? Have you photos of injuries? Have you recorded accurate data and had it verified so it will hold up when challenged? Did you record accurate testimony supporting any suspicious incidents?

Once you feel confidence with the evidence, can you list the reasons for your suspicion? What physical bruises, scars, or other signs have you observed? What behaviors have you seen in the adolescent that point to abuse or neglect? Can you identify some emotional indicators that led you to suspect maltreatment?

How much have you been able to observe the teenager's family? Have you noticed how they interact? What attitudes are evident in their treatment of family members? What qualities do the parents communicate to their children? In what way to extended family members affect the interpersonal dynamics?

Do other people suspect maltreatment? Have you discussed your suspicions with others who have an opportunity to see the evidence? If you are in a school system, for example, have you looked to teachers or the adolescent's bus driver or coach for confirmation of your suspicions? Think about other outsiders with whom this youth must come in contact regularly and consider in whom the teenager might have confided.

Where to File a Report

Do you have or know where to get the appropriate paper work and forms to file a report? If there are none, have you organized your records as fully as possible? If you are turning outside your organization or if you are an independent observer, what is the official procedure in your community or state? If you work for a community or educational organization, is there an appointed person responsible for filing official reports? Are there specific agencies with whom you should be dealing? When do you file the report? Have you the necessary information in written form and can you support it verbally? Can you document your case?

Finally, who will stand behind you if you do file your suspicions? If challenged on your motives, overzealousness, or other points, have you anyone who will testify in your behalf? Is there anyone else outside the family who is willing to corroborate your report?

There are many things to consider and many steps to take before filing an official report, but this doesn't mean help isn't needed. It is definitely a risk to turn in suspected abusers. However, by reporting the incidents you are providing a way for the adolescent and the perpetrator to get help. It is worth the effort, even when it isn't a clear-cut decision.

Reasons to Follow Through

There are at least three main reasons for following through with the report and for always making your decision in favor of the youth. Adolescent abuse is often masked by other problems such as running away, delinquency, truancy, or the use of drugs and alcohol. Others may not see through the behaviors to the source of the problem in this young person's life.

Also, many people don't know how to identify or interpret symptoms. They may see only the surface problems and may not care to or know how to look further.

Societal beliefs about privacy, parental power and appropriate behaviors color typical reactions. Common attitudes about adolescents create biases against reporting, especially those that ignore the behavior patterns that take root in childhood. A general tendency to blame the victims once they reach a certain size or age works against the youths' need for help.

Abused youths often encounter the juvenile court system before any other community agency. Many adolescents go through the entire judicial process without ever even being suspected as victims of abuse or neglect. Instead, teenagers are considered drug addicts, juvenile delinquents, or dropouts. Rather than being seen as symptoms of a greater problem, these dysfunctions become labels that poorly define the individuals and stick with them as they mature. The young people come to believe these things about themselves, having been set up for negative self-esteem through parental maltreatment.

These problems, however, are each large issues in and of themselves, separate from the abuse and neglect. Professionals and other community workers often don't consider abuse or neglect as possible causes of the adolescent's maladjustment. As a result, no investigation of the family is undertaken and no help is made available.

Teenagers Face Society's Stereotypes

Part of the battle in fighting adolescent abuse is conquering stereotypes or misconstrued assumptions. Society believes, for example, that the abuse of youth is primarily sexual. The public also fails to see adolescents as victims because they appear able to defend themselves, seek help, or run away. Since teenagers are bigger and stronger even than their parents may be, they are not seen as defenseless in the same way as infants and younger children are. Even the now-accepted battered spouse syndrome leaves teenagers out, although similar emotional and financial constraints operate to keep youths from retaliation or escape.

Observations are usually based on what we know, so people who believe they are familiar with the behavioral characteristics of the typical teenager may make the wrong assumptions about adolescents. They may see the symptoms and conclude that an abused or neglected youth is actually acting inappropriately for his or her age, is uncontrollable, or is a "normal" rebellious teenager. Youths who are shy or withdrawn also may be misjudged, with adults assuming it is their "normal" behavior.

Many adults who work with young people remain unaware of the symptoms of abuse and neglect. They may be looking only for physical evidence, but adolescents often show no obvious signs of abuse. The only indicator that something is wrong at home may be the teenager's behavior.

When a report has actually been filed and a caseworker shows up at the adolescent's home, the teenager may feel embarrassed, confused, scared, or relieved. Victims need to feel things will be okay. They need to know they have support and can get assistance when they need it. At the same time, teenagers need to vent the anger and frustration they inevitably feel toward the abuser. Some of this negative energy may be directed toward the people who tried to help by intervening, since the youth will still feel unsafe with those emotions at home.

At this point abused youths' self-esteem may need a boost. They may need to learn new methods of coping or to adjust their present coping methods to more appropriate behavior. They may have to learn how to focus their energy on more age-appropriate tasks. These new coping strategies should help the adolescents grow emotionally and physically. This can be encouraged by helping teenage victims to concentrate on their current strengths and interests. That teaches them to improve their existing skills, increases their self-esteem, and may even motivate them to work on additional areas of personal weakness.

Youths already considered incorrigible or disruptive may need more attention. It is important to reinforce their positive behaviors while teaching them responsibility for their actions. These adolescents also may need to learn to consider themselves worthy of any good things that come their way. They may have picked up the abusive behaviors of their parents and turned that attitude in on themselves. They may have to relearn how to talk to and treat themselves in a positive way.

Be There for the Adolescents

One of the best ways you can help these young victims after intervention is to assure them that they can rely on you. If you intend to be there for them, convince them you are available and willing to help when they need help and to listen when they need to talk. They need to know that you will understand what they're feeling and that you won't condemn them for it.

It is important that you not solve their problems for them, however. If they have been subjected to the immense control that usually exists in dysfunctional homes, then they may never have had to face their problems alone before. They may expect you to "fix" it for them and may resent it when you merely talk with them and try to help them learn how to take care of themselves. They desperately need a chance to discover functional, caring ways of coping and changing their lives.

A variety of agencies may work together at this point to assist the teenagers and their families. Some of these include:

Health Care

Providing health-care services is another positive avenue of intervention. Medical assistance can correct or rule out any physical problems stemming from abuse and neglect. Among the services available from these sources are health care screening, dental care, child-care clinics, birth control information, immunization, and referral.

One advantage available when health-care services are utilized is that the parents can be given information about the proper care of children and adolescents. These parents may actually not have known better. It has been shown that one cause of adolescent abuse and neglect stems from the existence of an unintended family via an unwanted, untimed pregnancy.

Dealing from a reality-based framework, these medical services should provide parents and adolescents with accurate, unbiased information about birth control methods. Clinics and classes make excellent sources for dissemination of information and related services. If pregnancy has already occurred, objective counseling should be available dealing with decisions about carrying the pregnancy to term, adoption, or parenting. Postnatal classes on child care and development should be offered.

A related issue is premature birth, more common among teenagers than more mature women. Young mothers with premature infants require instruction on how to provide the extra care these babies need in infancy and as they mature. Again, classes, workshops, or support groups are beneficial.

Mental Health

Most communities have some type of mental health services that are supported by government, private, or religious organizations. These agencies offer some form of counseling and support to individuals or entire families. Although they are available to those who request assistance, most abusive parents don't seek out counseling on their own. They are usually referred by other agencies to these centers for treatment or are ordered into treatment by the courts.

To intervene effectively, professionals should create public awareness of the services available. It should be made clear that these are of a supportive rather than intrusive nature and that the counseling is available during a crisis. The public needs to understand that these services are nonblaming, and that they are geared to bring a sense of "normalcy" to individual lives. It is important to communicate that taking advantage of mental health services can help families and individuals resolve conflicts before they lead to abuse and neglect. Above all, public and private services should appear nonthreatening and nonjudgmental.

Parent Education

Another form of intervention comes from classes that teach parenting skills ranging from conflict resolution to cooking. Parent education provides information while giving adults a chance to meet other people and make friends who are developing similar positive goals and outlooks on life.

This support can temper feelings of isolation and help increase the parents' use of social skills.

Information taught in these sessions includes new discipline or leadership techniques, preparation of balanced meals and nutrition, how to budget money, and effective coping strategies. The classes should address general skills that can be applied to several situations and skills that are positive aspects to parenting.

It is common for students to follow the suggestions in detail rather than catching the intent and the spirit of the communication. This occurs because dysfunctional parents may not know how to be flexible or inventive with their existing skills. It may be necessary to give several examples of practical application and to stress that what worked for one family may not work the same way for another. Parents should understand that each family and its circumstances are somewhat unique, although the commonality of everyone's situations must be acknowledged.

What these parents need to see is that it is okay if they have to try a different technique to solve the same problem experience by another family. No single technique works all the time, but different techniques work at different times. It is this ability to make selective choices that needs to be taught, giving parents the ability to let go of blame when some technique doesn't work once, and yet to go on to try something else. They also need not to discard one method simply because it didn't serve the need in a single application.

215

Financial Assistance

Abuse and neglect may have occurred due to financial stress. Not having enough money to make ends meet or a sudden, unexpected decrease in income can cause even the best parents to lose confidence in their parenting ability. They may feel embarrassed, helpless, angry, or frustrated themselves. Unemployment benefits eventually run out. What public assistance is available may not be enough to feed and clothe growing adolescents when the cost of that is added to other household expenses.

It is impossible for a community to give direct financial support to everyone who is unemployed or receives welfare. However, there are other ways to help. Food banks, clothing drives and fund-raisers provide profits and essential items for the needy.

Assistance also may take the form of job-training classes to increase employment skills or to teach clients how to search for a job. Some communities may have job banks available for public use. Parents may lack the skills to get a better job and may have no money to afford career training. Grants, scholarships, and public programs can offer vocational training to the disadvantaged, giving parents an opportunity to better themselves. Of course, those that include child care in these services have a higher success rate since the cost of baby-sitters or the risk of leaving youngsters alone may outweigh the parents' motivation to work for change.

Often both parents in a financially strapped family don't work precisely because they can't afford child care. It may, indeed, be more economical for one parent to stay home with the children even though other opportunities must be ignored.

This is part of the cycle that perpetuates the problem. Parents whose earning potential is limited to minimum wage cannot afford to pay fifty dollars or more per child per week for nursery school. Because they need to keep costs low to survive, day-care centers are forced to pay minimum wages to their employees. Trained educators or professional child-care workers find themselves unable to improve their financial status by dedicating themselves to their profession, so they move on. The children in these schools suffer as less skilled, lower-paid workers come in. Quality is reduced, setting the children up for poorer school performance and by that sentencing them to educational disadvantages. Only outside funds or a change in society's priorities concerning child care and family issues will make the difference.

While adolescents may need less supervision than pre-schoolers, the need for structured, supervised activities for teenagers is just as strong. Parents are even less inclined to spend precious dollars on what they perceive as baby-sitting for their youths. They may already be relying on the teenagers to supervise their younger brothers and sisters, especially if the parents work evenings.

It is safe for most teenagers to stay alone for short periods of time, but those left without some supervised or structured activities are likely to lose interest in appropriate activities. Community dollars are well spent when directing youth to positive organizations such as scouting, activity centers, boys' or girls' clubs, sports, and recreation for both genders or other groups. Even encouraging some part-time employment for older teenagers may be more positive than simply leaving them home alone where boredom leads directly to trouble.

Community Outreach

Intervention may involve community outreach services such as professional homemakers, social workers, self-help groups and youth resources. Homemakers come into the home and help parents shop, clean house, cook and do other domestic tasks. Because they help families directly, homemakers may be the most beneficial in situations of neglect. These people give the family a model of how to run a household appropriately and how to handle everyday situations adequately.

Social workers "provide mediation of disputes, referral services, counseling, recreation programming and implementation" to youth and families within a given area. These persons work to strengthen family ties by building self-esteem and mutual respect among individuals. They involve professionals, volunteers, and peers. They meet a variety of family needs in a variety of ways, so getting information out about what is available may be the first step in utilization of these services.

Self-help groups can serve both adults and youths. Many are organized around the principles of popular Twelve-Step Programs that originated through organizations like Alcoholics Anonymous. Adult self-help groups such as

Parents Anonymous, Parents United, Adult Children of Alcoholics, Codependents Anonymous, and others speak to the individual's specific issues while taking a nonjudgmental view of society's dysfunctional families. They can be located through the telephone book, newspaper calendars, or referral agencies. The strength of these groups is that they help adults learn about themselves, find mutual support, and adopt positive coping skills.

Sometimes adult groups will meet at the same time as those for children or youth. Some organizations that serve teenagers in the same manner as the adult groups are Daughters and Sons United and Alateen. These provide educational information to help adolescents understand their parents and suggest ways for the parents to deal with the family's problems. They also focus on the teenagers' personal feelings about what is happening within their family and offer a nonjudgmental atmosphere where the youths can explore themselves.

What Self-Help Groups Do

There are at least four purposes for youth self-help groups. They provide a supportive setting where teenagers can talk with other adolescents going through similar experiences. They can discuss the effectiveness of their coping strategies and learn new ones that work. Through these organizations teenagers find support for seeking intervention. Finally, they teach skills that prevent the young people involved from continuing their parents' patterns and becoming abusers when they themselves form adult relationships or become parents.

This is one reason why these groups may concentrate on parenting skills, conflict resolution, and appropriate roles for teenagers. The young people learn what behaviors are acceptable or productive for adults and about human developmental patterns.

One of the greatest benefits for teenagers in self-help groups is that they are encouraged to share their feelings. They have a forum where they can tell others what they think about and what they feel without fearing repercussions. They learn how to communicate openly with others.

Some youth resources are organized and run by teenagers themselves. These range from peer-staffed hotlines and self-help groups to pamphlets and public awareness campaigns. These activities are all carried out completely by the young people involved, including the design and writing of the printed material or the organization of publicity.

Recreation

Adolescents have a normal and healthy need for adventure and risk-taking that can be successfully channeled into recreational programs. Adult and youth activities are usually offered through public parks, religious centers and recreational and sports programs.

Physical activity helps relieve stress and frustration. Sports and recreational activities also give participants a way to socialize in a positive environment. Participation on teams or in other recreational activities may alleviate teenagers' feelings of isolation while teaching them to work with others toward a common goal.

These kinds of activities also may open other doors for isolated young people. For the first time, outside a forced academic atmosphere, they may interact and find themselves joining efforts with individuals of varying races, ethnic origins, economic status and lifestyles. They may begin to examine their issues on an unconscious level as they break through the myths of racism, ageism, homophobia, sexism, ableism, and other forms of discrimination.

On another level, participating in sports or other leisure activities may give these youths their first sincere experience with laughter and fun. That alone may be enough to let the healing begin.

Summary

Reporting can begin the dysfunctional family's healing process. Standards for reporting, with recognizable risk profiles need to be developed. These must be understood by those who file reports. However, when professionals intervene in the existing abusive or neglectful situation, those involved must seek new ways of relating, coping and taking care of themselves.

Adolescent victims especially need to know there are people whom they can trust. It is likely they have poor self-esteem or may already be showing signs of juvenile delinquency. They will need convincing that others care. At the same time, the entire family needs practical help as well as education. When financial, medical, recreational and psychological needs are met, the first steps toward recovery will be underway.

13

Conclusion

A complex web of economic, social, and cultural factors interact to create an environment where abuse and neglect are not only allowed to exist, but even sometimes are condoned by society. None of the adverse conditions that reinforce the problem can be treated effectively in isolation from the others. In every case, the causes and effects of abuse and neglect differ.

Somewhere on the invisible continuum connecting healthy parenting with severe abuse and neglect is a boundary beyond which society will no longer tolerate maltreatment of children and adolescents. This is a moveable point, redefined over generations and as more is learned about the human psyche and developmental stages. All those who act on their feelings, lack control of their impulses, or are confused about their responsibilities in life are not abusive parents. Others who have been consistently effective parents may occasionally slip into irresponsibility, negativity, or physical punishment.

The fact that this boundary of acceptability is moveable is important to note, just as it is vital to acknowledge that no stereotypes, and no assumptions based on statistics or cultural values can be taken as truth. Many single, teenage, or economically poor parents never abuse or neglect their offspring. Families who live an unconventional lifestyle may be more healthy than the white, middle-class Protestant nuclear family next door. Children who have been victims of abuse or neglect do not necessarily grow up to perpetuate the maltreatment with their own youngsters or partners. Some do.

Research is Essential

If the problem of adolescent abuse and neglect is so complex, you may wonder what can really be done to combat it. How can prevention and intervention efforts become more effective?

Healing our society of abuse and neglect begins with research. We need research not only to find the extent and nature of existing adolescent abuse, but also to help us develop usable definitions distinguishing between the types of abuse and neglect.

Communication is a vital link in this, since research that is not known about is of little use. It has been said that "the effectiveness of the abuse/neglect system is largely dependent on the functioning of each part within the system, and the ability of those parts to work together toward a common goal."

Agencies Need More Awareness

Moving in this direction, agencies need to be aware of their roles and responsibilities in relationship to solving the problem. There needs to be a format of interagency relationships and an exchange of interagency information. If these things can happen, there is a chance that the performance of the existing abuse/neglect prevention and intervention systems would improve dramatically.

This success also depends on the resources available in each community. Different parts of the nation and the world offer different levels of support based largely on the area's economy. However, if we consider these issues in terms of emotional ecology, then we will realize that healing only one town or one state will be no more effective in making change than a placing a Band-Aid over a broken leg. It is necessary to provide funds and large scale resources for local agencies for services that are aware not only of their fight against abuse and neglect but also of their responsibility to work with others to provide the best possible services to those who need them.

Besides having the resources (financial, practical, and educational) to provide needed services, those working with abuse and neglect cases need to be aware of the extensive dynamics involved. They should be knowledgeable about the causes, effects, indicators and family systems. They should be trained to deal with the crises they

225

will face when working with these dysfunctional, hurting families.

Professionals directly involved in cases are not the only ones who need this education. Public awareness is invaluable. Anyone can encounter an abusive or neglectful situation in one's neighborhood, at the grocery, on the street, at one's place of worship, or in a hospital. Nonprofessionals whose work brings them into contact with adolescents need to know the whole story behind teenage behavior.

Everyone Needs to Know

Because every person is a potential resource, information about how to report cases of suspected abuse and neglect should be distributed to every citizen. Agencies that provide services need to build a high profile so that concerned individuals are aware of the problems, know what to do and where to turn for help. They also need information about how to be supportive rather than perpetuating the problems.

Naturally, procedures used in prevention sometimes overlap with those used in intervention. The same methods may be effective for interrupting destructive family patterns as for preventing recurrence of abuse or neglect. They involve increasing knowledge, educational encouragement, conflict resolution abilities, and parenting skills. Positive change is reinforced by support groups, health care, and community involvement.

Selection of the most appropriate type of intervention or prevention for a particular case depends on such factors as available funds, the willingness of agencies to participate and cooperate, the motivation of family members to get involved, the willingness of agencies to change policies and procedures to permit accepting cases of adolescent maltreatment, and the amount of support available from the community and other professionals.

Consider Community Needs

The total needs of each community also must be considered when deciding upon the approach that best fits a particular situation. When determining this, questions to ask include:

- Who is the at-risk population?

- Who needs the greatest amount of help?

- What type of aid would be most beneficial?

- What are the issues involved with each approach that is being considered?

- What are the characteristics of the people who would be involved with such an effort?

- What are the needs of adolescents?

- What services already exist?

- Can these services meet any of the needs or do program adjustments need to be made?

- Are agencies willing to adjust?

- What new services can be offered?

- What services would the at-risk population prefer?

Networking Works

It would be impossible to address all these issues when developing programs for intervention and prevention. To be sure that important issues are not overlooked, the best way to deal with the problem of adolescent abuse and neglect may be to form a network. Professionals, paraprofessionals, community workers, family members in recovery, political leaders, and others need to work together to understand and approach the issues. Each would have a specific role in the network. Each would deal with certain issues, try to resolve them, and have the support of the group when programs are initiated. The network would also be there to implement the program's goals.

To combat effectively adolescent abuse and neglect, ideas and resources of all those involved must be brought together in the open. One organization alone cannot resolve all the issues and problems. Preventing and intervening in these cases must involve a combined effort. Although each community will want to decide how it will handle the problem on a local level, programs must maintain a sensitivity and commitment to the people served.

Abusive and neglectful families lack the internal and external support systems normally available to others. The low self-esteem of family members often interferes with efforts to help them change their lives. Because of their previous failures and lack of belief in themselves, these families are often stigmatized by society, thus eliminating external support and further reinforcing their poor sense of worth.

Help in creating these missing support mechanisms is vital. Services need to focus on strengthening the self-defined family unit and furthering the development of positive relationships between adolescents and their families. Therefore, those selected to work with these cases must be able to "love, support, parent and empathize with abusive and neglectful families." They need to be able to deal with anger, hostility, rejection, and overcompliance. Because they are constantly on the front line where they are required to become involved in the day-to-day family issues, they themselves need continual emotional reinforcement. They need supervisors who are understanding and supportive, encouraging the workers' right to be flexible and creative in their work.

Prevention Can Improve Quality of Life

The main theme behind prevention and intervention is improving the quality of life for all families. People need an opportunity if they are to make positive change. They

229

need a positive, supportive environment in which to recognize their need for change and to undertake the challenging process.

Before change can occur, individuals must have a desire for change, the energy to sustain it and the resources to support it. Change is not the responsibility of one person alone, but of everyone involved. Family members, professionals, friends, neighbors, and relatives are needed to support these efforts.

Prevention of and intervention in cases of adolescent abuse and neglect is the shared responsibility of the whole community. It is as much a part of the interdependent web of life as the ecosystem and the atmosphere. Human emotional ecology cannot be limited to one family, one city, one state, or one nation. To change one life may be to change them all.

Notes on Sources

There are many individuals and publications whose ideas have contributed to this book. While it is impossible to credit everyone whose work, writings or philosophical perspectives have influenced the creation of *Too Old to Cry*, this is an attempt to list the major influences on the development of the authors' perspective. Hopefully, this effort will give the reader a basis for a broader insight into the issues presented here and a guide for further study.

Chapter 1.
Hitting Home: Tapped Teens in Abusive Families

3   THE TRUTH IS These statistics are quoted from an article by Casey Banas published in the *Chicago Tribune* April 8, 1990. They are from the first national

study of eighth graders done by the National Center for Education Statistics.

6 CHILD MALTREATMENT IS NOT This information is drawn from significant work by Mayhall, P.D.
and Norgard, K.E., 1983. *Child Abuse and Neglect*. New
York: John Wiley and Sons.

7 THOSE CHILDREN WHO SURVIVED Robert L.
Hampton looks beyond surface assumptions to explore
the reasons behind and implications of abusive black
families. Rather than ignoring the inherent inequality
of patriarchal society, he examines real cultural and
racist connections of non-white dysfunctional families.
Much information and insight was drawn from his
book, *Violence in the Black Family*, 1987, Lexington,
Massachusetts: Lexington Books, D.C. Heath and
Company.

8 MANY SUCH JUDGMENT CALLS These facts are
from work by M.A. Thomas, 1977, *Children Alone:
What can be done about abuse and neglect?* It was
published by the Virginia Council for Exceptional
Children.

9 THE PRECISE NUMBER These statistical estimates
are drawn from work by B. Roscoe and K.L. Peterson,
1983, Parents of battered and neglected children: What
child care providers should know, published in the
Journal of Child Care, 1(5), 674-6832. Also included are
figures from work by J. Wilson, D. Thomas and L.
Shuette, 1983, The silent scream: Recognizing abused
children, *Education*, 104 (1), 100-103. Also from R.E.

Helfer, 1982, in a review of the literature on the prevention of child abuse and neglect, *Child Abuse and Neglect: The International Journal*, 6, 251-926. In Lutzker, J.R., Wesch, D. and Rice, J.M., 1984, a review of the project '12-ways': An ecobehavioral approach to the treatment and prevention of child abuse and neglect. *Advances in Behavior Research and Therapy*, 6(1), 63-73.

9   SADLY, THE NUMBER OF REPORTED Information presented here is backed up by several researchers. Mayhall and Norgard, 1983, R.W. Blum and C. Runyan, 1980, Adolescent abuse: The dimensions of the problem, *Journal of Adolescent Health Care*, 1, 121-126. Also B. Fisher, J. Berdie, J. Cook and N. Day, 1980, *Adolescent abuse and neglect: Intervention strategies*, U.S. Department of Health and Human Services, Office of Human Development Services, Administration for Children, Youth and Families, Children's Bureau, National Center on Child Abuse and Neglect, D.M. Paperny and R.W. Deischer, 1983, Maltreatment of adolescents: The relationship to a predisposition toward violent behavior and delinquency, *Adolescence*, 18, 499-506.

10   IN CONTRAST, ADOLESCENTS These observations are verified by K. Hoekstra, 1984, Ecologically defining the mistreatment of adolescents, *Children and Youth Services Review*, 6, 285-293. And Thomas, 1977.

10   TEENAGERS ARE LIKELY VICTIMS The basically powerless position of adolescents in today's society is made clear in work by B. Fisher, J. Berdie, J. Cook and

N. Day, 1980, *Adolescent Abuse and Neglect: Intervention Strategies*, U.S. Department of Health and Human Services, Office of Human Development Services, Administration for Children, Youth and Families, Children's Bureau, National Center on Child Abuse and Neglect. Also by Thomas, 1977.

CHAPTER 2.
What Makes This Family Different: Defining Values

20 IT IS POSSIBLE From Mayhall and Norgard, 1983.

21 BESIDES THE NEW. Jay Belsky gives an in-depth look at factors and characteristics many abusive families have in common. Some generalizations can be made, although not every case will reflect the same situations or influences. This information is available in "Child Maltreatment and the Emergent Family System," published in the book *Early Prediction and Prevention of Child Abuse*, 1988, edited by Kevin Browne, Cliff Davies and Peter Stratton, 1988, New York: John Wiley and Sons, Ltd.

22 NEIGHBORHOODS ARE SURPRISINGLY Also from Belsky, 1988.

25 MEMBERS OF NONABUSING FAMILIES Sources for this section include Mayhall and Norgard, 1983; and A.C. Serrano, M.B. Zuelzer, D.D. Howe and R.E. Reposa, 1980, Ecology of abusive and nonabusive families: Implications for intervention, *Advances in Family Psychiatry*, 2, 183-195.

25 HEALTHY FAMILIES AREN'T AFRAID From Serrano, et al., 1980.

26 LACK OF SUPPORT Background on these dynamics at work are available in an article by D. Graybill and C.A. Davis, 1983, Comparison of family environment of abused vs. nonabused children, *Psychology: A Quarterly Journal of Human Behavior*, 20(1), 34-37.

26 THE DIFFERENCE BETWEEN These comparisons are drawn from work of F.G. Bolton, Director of Human Services, Arizona Community Development for Abuse and Neglect, D.E.S., as quoted in work by P.D. Mayhall and K.E. Norgard, 1983, *Child Abuse and Neglect*, New York: John Wiley and Sons.

27 SIMPLY LIVING AS From Robert L. Hampton, *Violence in the Black Family*, 1987.

29 THERE IS A TRAP Observations on motivation taken from Ray Hoskins' book *Rational Madness*, 1989, Human Services Institute, Bradenton, Florida and Tab Books, Inc., Blue Ridge Summit, Pennsylvania.

30 IT IS VITALLY From Serano et al., 1980.

30 WHILE THESE FACTORS From Mayhall and Norgard, 1983.

CHAPTER 3.
Parents Who Abuse: Misplaced Violence

38 PARENTS WHO RESORT TO Guidelines taken from work by C.C. Towers, 1984, in *Child Abuse and Neglect: A teacher's handbook for detection, reporting and classroom management*, Washington, D.C., National Education Association.

41 FAILING TO DEAL WITH Direct Information as well as personal insight was gained from Michael Popkin's course and book, *Active Parenting: Teaching, Cooperation, Courage and Responsibility*, 1987, New York, Harper and Row, Publishers. Special personal insight was added by Suzanne Gellens, 1989 president of the Florida Association for Children Under Six and a trained Active Parenting instructor in Sarasota, Florida.

50 NATURALLY, NOT ALL Information from a variety of sources were combined to supply common characteristics of abusive families. Those whose work was used as reference here include A. Brenner, 1984, *Helping children cope with stress*, Massachusetts: Lexington Books, Also, M. Halpern, 1979, *Helping maltreated children*, St. Louis, CV Mosby Company. Mayhall and Norgard, 1983. B. Pianta, 1984, Antecedents of child abuse: Single and multiple factor models, *School Psychology International*, 5, 151-160. Roscoe and Peterson, 1983. M.S. Rosenberg and N.D. Repucci, 1983, Abusive mothers: Perceptions of their own children's behavior, *Journal of Consulting and Clinical Psychology*, 51(5), 674-682. Towers, 1984.

50 THERE ARE MANY WAYS Factors cited by Roscoe and Peterson, 1983.

52 ABUSE FOLLOWS AS Taken from Rosenberg and Reppucci, 1983, p. 674.

53 SOME PARENTS VIEW From Towers, 1984.

CHAPTER 4.
Sins of Omission: Parents Who Neglect

61 IF NEGLECT OCCURS A helpful and insightful perspective as well as factual information was obtained for this section from Jane Middleton-Moz in a 1990 workshop in Sarasota, Florida and from her book *Shame and Guilt: Masters of Disguise*, 1990, Deerfield Beach, Florida: Health Communications Inc.

64 NEGLECTFUL PARENTS HAVE MANY Drawn from Towers, 1984.

68 FINANCIAL NEEDS CAN CAUSE This information was complied from a variety of sources. They include Brenner, 1984, and Halpern, 1979. Also W.J. Junewicz, 1983. A protective posture toward emotional neglect and abuse, *Child Welfare*, 62(3), 243-252; Mayhall and Norgard, 1983; Roscoe and Peterson, 1983.

68 NEGLECTFUL PARENTS SOMETIMES From Brenner, 1984.

69 ANOTHER COMMON TRAIT This comes from R.G. Burgess and R.D. Conger, 1978, Family interactions in abusive, neglectful and normal families, *Child Development*, 49, 1163-1173.

70 ALL THESE BEHAVIORS From Fisher, *et al.*, 1980. Also, J. Garbarino and G. Gilliam, 1980, *Understanding abusive families*, Massachusetts: Lexington Books; Mahall and Norgard, 1983.

71 CHILDREN SEE THEMSELVES From Fisher, *et al.*, 1980; Middleton-Moz, 1990.

71 DIFFERENT RELIGIOUS, ETHNIC Additional information from Hampton, 1987.

73 FINALLY, THE NEGLECTFUL PARENTS Also from Mayhall and Norgard, 1983.

73 THE THIRD TYPE OF ADOLESCENT From Fisher, *et al.*, 1990; Mayhall and Norgard, 1983.

74 SIMILARLY, THIS PATTERN OF NEGLECT Fisher, *et al.*, 1980; Mayhall and Norgard, 1983.

CHAPTER 5.
Why Do They Hurt Me? Causes of Adolescent Abuse

81 ALTHOUGH THERE ARE PLENTY From Blum and Runyun, 1980; Thomas, 1977.

81 ADOLESCENCE IS ALSO A TIME Fisher, *et al.*, 1980.

81 AT THIS TIME OF PERSONAL From Hoekstra, 1984.

82 PROBLEMS ARISE, HOWEVER Additional information drawn from Blum and Runyun, 1980; Hoekstra, 1984; Thomas, 1977.

84 AS TEENAGERS BEGIN TO IMITATE Again, Garbarino and Gilliam, 1980.

86 THE RESULTS CAN BE WORSE Serious implications of the growing threat of teenage suicide are explored in depth by Philip G. Patros and Tonia K. Shamoo in their book, *Depression and Suicide in Children and Adolescents: Prevention, Intervention and Postvention*, 1989, Needham Heights, Massachusetts, Allyn and Bacon Inc, a division of Simon and Schuster.

CHAPTER 6.
Effects of Abuse and Neglect: What Happens After?

95 PHYSICALLY ABUSED CHILDREN From Mayhall & Norgard, 1983.

95 VICTIMS OF ABUSE AND NEGLECT. Symptoms compiled from various resources including Fisher, *et al.*, 1980; N.L. Galambos & R.A. Dixon, 1984, Adolescent abuse and the development of personal sense of control, *Child Abuse and Neglect*, 8, 285-293; J. Garbarino and A.C. Garbarino, 1982, *Maltreatment of Adolescents*, National Committee for Prevention of Child Abuse.

96 JUST AS INDIVIDUALS More specific understanding of the dynamics and difficulties of mothers as victims of abusive spouses can be gained by reading *Abused No More: Recovery for Women from Abusive and Co-Dependent Relationships*, 1989, Human Services Institute, Bradenton, Florida, and Tab Books Inc., Blue Ridge Summit, Pa. Also in one of the first books on the subject, *Battered Wives* by Del Martin, 1981, San Francisco, California: Volcano Press.

98 THESE YOUNG PEOPLE ARE TOTALLY From Ackerman and Pickering, 1989.

98 ANXIETY IS CLOSELY RELATED From Garbarino & Gilliam, 1980.

99 FEELING OVERLY DEPENDENT From S. Bavelok, D. Kline, J. McLaughlin and P. Publicover, 1979, Primary prevention of child abuse and neglect: Identification of high risk adolescents, *Child Abuse and Neglect*, 3, 1071-1080, as quoted in N.L. Galambos and R.A. Dixon, 1984, Adolescent abuse and the development of personal sense of control, *Child Abuse and Neglect*, 8, 285-293. Also from Brenner, 1984.

100 OTHER TECHNIQUES FOR ESCAPING For specific information on teenage runaways, consult T. Houten and M. Golembiewski, 1976, A study of runaway youth and their families, Youth Alternative Project, Washington, D.C., as cited in N.L. Galambos and R.A. Dixon, 1984.

101 MORE THAN ONE THOUSAND Information from Philip G. Patros and Tonia K. Shamoo, 1989.

102 DELINQUENCY, THE LACK OF Connections between teenage delinquency and adolescent abuse are made clearly by Garbarino & Garbarino, 1982; Paperny & Deischer, 1983; Thomas, 1977.

102 WHEN DELINQUENT BEHAVIORS From Garbarino & Garbarino, 1982.

102 THE HIGH LEVELS OF FEAR From Thomas, 1977.

102 ANXIETY MAY ALSO Sources of anxiety and shame are explained in detail by Middleton-Moz, 1990. Also drawn from Paperny & Deischner, 1983.

103 AGAIN, ADOLESCENTS WHO Retrieved from Bender, 1957, What are influential factors that predispose the youth of our society to delinquency and crime? In F. Cohen (ed.), *Youth and Crime*, New York: International University Press.

103 VICTIMS OF ABUSE HAVE SEVERAL Also from Brenner, 1984.

104 SOMETIMES VICTIMS WANT Brenner, 1984.

CHAPTER 7.
Recognizing the Danger: Signs of Abuse

108 AN ABUSED OR NEGLECTED CHILD From Fisher, *et al.*, 1980, p. 1.

109 TECHNICALLY, PHYSICAL ABUSE From Mayhall & Norgard, 1983, p. 100.

109 THOSE CONCERNED ABOUT ABUSED These signs of physical abuse were compiled from Fisher, *et al.*, 1980; Halpern, 1979; Mayhall & Norgard, 1983; Towers, 1984; Wilson, Thomas & Shuette, 1983.

112 SOME TRENDS, HOWEVER Hampton, 1987, p.15.

114 SPECIFIC BEHAVIORAL SIGNS Fisher, et al., 1980; Halpern, 1979; Towers, 1984; Wilson, Thomas and Shuette, 1983.

116 MOST ADOLESCENTS DISPLAY M. Lauderdale, A. Valinas and M. Anderson, 1989, "Race, Ethnicity, and Child Maltreatment; An Empirical Analysis," *Child Abuse and Neglect* 4, No. 3:163-169 as quoted in Hampton, 1987.

116 WHILE MOST AUTHORITY FIGURES Also from Hampton, 1987.

118 ALTHOUGH OTHER MINORITIES R.A. Dubanoski and K. Snyder, 1980, "Patterns of Child Abuse and Neglect in Japanese and Samoan-Americans," *Child*

Abuse and Neglect 5, No. 4:457-466; Lauderdale, et al., 1980, both in Hampton, 1987.

118 NON-ANGLO CULTURES Towers, 1984.

122 ELEVEN FAMILY DYNAMICS Mayhall and Norgard, 1983.

CHAPTER 8.
Subtle Symptoms: Spotting Neglect

127 ONE DEFINITION OF NEGLECT From I. Wolock and B. Horowitz, 1984, Child Maltreatment as a Social Problem: The Neglect of Neglect, *American Journal of Othopsychiatry*, 54(4), 530-543.

128 EVENTUALLY THESE YOUNG PEOPLE Halpern, 1979.

129 BEHAVIOR, HOWEVER, OFFERS From Brenner, 1984.

131 IF THE PARENTS THEMSELVES Brenner, 1984; Halpern, 1979; Mayhall & Norgard, 1983.

132 THESE ARE PHYSICAL SIGNS From Brenner, 1984; Fisher, *et al.*, 1980; Roscoe and Peterson, 1983; Towers, 1984.

134 OTHER EMOTIONAL INDICATORS Roscoe and Peterson, 1983.

135 THESE ARE CERTAIN BEHAVIORAL Compiled from Halpern, 1979; Thomas, 1977; Towers, 1984.

136 INDEED, THESE YOUNG PEOPLE From Roscoe and Peterson, 1983.

136 THERE ARE QUALITIES OF Fisher, et al., 1980.

138 CHILDREN AND ADOLESCENTS WHOSE Referenced again from Ackerman and Pickering, 1989.

CHAPTER 9.
What's Being Done: Coping With the Problem

147 MANY COMMUNITIES Mayhall & Norgard, 1983.

147 CHILD PROTECTION TEAMS Mayhall & Norgard, 1983.

149 BEFORE CPS CLOSES THE BOOKS Selected information from J.L. Jenkins, M.K. Salus and G.L. Shultze, 1979, *Child Protective Services: A guide for workers*, Washington, D.C.: DHEW Publication (OHDS) 79-30103, in Mayhall and Norgard, 1983.

151 ACCORDING TO DR. GEORGE COMMERCI Also from Mayhall & Norgard, 1983, p. 216.

152 ANOTHER FACTOR THAT Mayhall & Norgard, 1983.

155 FINALLY, PARTICIPANTS WORK Brenner, 1984.

155 WHEN DEALING WITH ADOLESCENTS   Garbarino & Gilliam, 1980.

157 WHEN THE TEENAGERS' NEED Specific conclusions are taken from David N. Sandberg's book, *The Child Abuse-Delinquency Connection*, 1989, Massachusetts: Lexington Books.

157 MANY OTHER ISSUES Referenced from B. Fisher and J. Berdie, 1978, Adolescent abuse and neglect: Issues of incidence, intervention and service delivery. *Child Abuse and Neglect*, 2, 173-192.

158 EDUCATION IN ADOLESCENT ISSUES   From Halpern, 1979.

158 ANY FUTURE EFFORTS TOWARD From Fisher and Berdie, 1978.

161 ONE EXAMPLE OF A COMMUNITY This profile of an alternative, intentional community where adolescents have an integral role in daily life comes from an interview with Mary Ellen Bower, Director of the Farm High School and a former chairperson of the National Coalition of Alternative Community Schools. The Farm is located in Summerville, Tennesssee.

CHAPTER 10.
Understanding Prevention & Intervention

168 OF COURSE, EVEN WHEN Information taken from
N.B. Ebling and D.A. Hill, 1975, *Child Abuse: Intervention and Treatment*, Massachusetts: Publishing Science
Group Inc.

169 SECONDARY PREVENTION INVOLVES Drawn
from work by N. Gilbert, 1982, Policy Issues in Primary
Prevention, *Social Work*, 27(4), 293-297. Also, H.J.
Staulcup and T.D. Royer, 1983, *The Development of
Preventative Methods in Child Welfare*, Children and
Youth Services, 5, 31-47.

170 THE THIRD STEP Gilbert, 1982, p. 293.

172 A COST-BENEFIT ANALYSIS This perspective was
taken from an interview with Suzanne Gellens, president of the Florida Association for Children Under Six,
where she quoted from a study called *Information
Changed Lives: The Effects of the Perry Preschool
Program on Youths Through Age 19*, Ypsilanti, Michigan. This research also backed the original creation
and implementation of the federal Head Start Program
in the United States.

176 INTERESTINGLY, PLACES OF EDUCATION
Comments from J. Garbarino, 1979, The Role of the
School in the Human Ecology of Child Maltreatment,
School Review, 87 (Feb.), 190-213.

176 BECAUSE SCHOOLS   Facts gathered from the American Humane Association, 1977, Annual report of the national clearinghouse on child abuse and neglect, Denver, Colorado: American Humane Association, as quoted in Garbarion and Gilliam, 1980.

176 EDUCATORS AND OTHERS   Information drawn from M. Soeffing, 1975, Abused Children are Exceptional Children, *Exceptional Children*, 42, 129, as appearing in Garbarino and Gilliam, 1980.

176 EDUCATION IN THE UNITED STATES   Statistics compiled by the Education Commission of the States, 1976, Child Abuse and Neglect Project, Education Policies and Practices Regarding Child Abuse and Neglect and Recommendations for Policy Development, p. 3, Denver, Colorado: Education Commission of the States, Report #8, as appearing in Garbarino and Gilliam, 1980.

176 ALTHOUGH EDUCATORS J. Delaney, 1976, New Concepts of the Family Court, p. 342, in R. Hefler and C.H. Kempe's *Child Abuse and Neglect: The Family and the Community*, Massachusetts: Ballinger.

177 THE SCHOOL SYSTEM   Drawn from R. Hefler, 1976, Basic Issues Concerning Predictions, p. 370, in Hefler and Kempe, 1976.

177 THE SCHOOL UTILIZING   Taken from research by E. Zigler, 1976, Controlling Child Abuse in America: An effort doomed to failure? Quoted in R. Burne

and E. Newberger, 1979, *Critical Perspectives on Child Abuse*, Massachusetts: Lexington Books.

178 IN TRUTH, THE FIRST ROLE Garbarino, 1979.

179 TEACHERS SEE THE SAME Information from G.M. Gardner, M. Schadler and S. Kemper, 1984, Classification Strategies Used by Mandated Reporters in Judging Incidents of Child Abuse, *Journal of Clinical Child Psychology*, 13(3), 280-287.

181 CURRENTLY, MANY TEACHERS Taken from A. Hazzard, 1984, Training Teachers to Identify and Intervene with Abused Children, *Journal of Clinical Child Psychology*, 13(3), 288-293.

CHAPTER 11.
What Can I Do? Making Change

186 THIS IS NOT AN EASY TASK Fisher, *et al.*, 1980.

186 ONE WAY TO HANDLE THIS Information gained from research by L.D. Chamblin and H.T. Prout, 1983, School Counselor and Reporting of Child Abuse: A survey of state laws and practices, *School Counselor*, 30(5), 358-367, Also, Towers, 1984.

187 PARENTS WHOSE HOME LIFE Thomas, 1977.

188 THE FOLLOWING EIGHT GUIDELINES From Halpern, 1979.

190 OPTIMAL CONDITIONS Towers, 1984.

192 ATTEMPTS TO PREVENT ADOLESCENT Additional information from Garbarino and Gilliam, 1980, p. 218.

193 A FIRST STEP IN THIS PROCESS Also Garbarino and Gilliam, 1980.

195 THE AVAILABILITY OF PROFESSIONAL From Garbarino & Gilliam, 1980.

196 WHILE EXTERNAL SUPPORT From Garbarino and Gilliam, 1980.

198 CHILDREN OF TEENAGE MOTHERS Data drawn from work by S.H. Miller, 1984, The Relationship Between Adolescent Child Bearing and Child Maltreatment, *Child Welfare*, 63(6), 553-557.

CHAPTER 12.
Intervention: When to Make the Move

202 FIRST AND MOST IMPORTANT Taken from S. Knapp, 1983, Counselor Liability for Failing to Report Child Abuse, *Elementary School Guidance and Counseling*, 17, 177-179. Also Towers, 1984.

202 ONE ISSUE CONCERNING CURRENT Taken from work by Kevin Brown, Cliff Davies, Peter Stratton, Early Prediction and Prevention of Child Abuse, 1988.

206 IF YOU FEEL YOU NEED TO FILE Modified from Towers, 1984, p. 43.

209 SOCIETAL BELIEFS ABOUT PRIVACY Fisher, *et al.*, 1980.

210 PART OF THE BATTLE IN FIGHTING Fisher, *et al.*, 1980. More in-depth treatment is also available by Maria Roy in her book, *Children in the Crossfire*, 1988, Deerfield Beach, Florida: Health Communications Inc.

213 PROVIDING HEALTH CARE More from Mayhall & Norgard, 1983; Fisher, *et al.*, 1980.

218 INTERVENTION MAY INVOLVE Mayhall & Norgard, 1983.

218 SOCIAL WORKERS PROVIDE Mayhall & Norgard, 1983, p. 300.

CHAPTER 13.
Conclusion

223 A COMPLEX WEB From Mayhall & Norgard, 1983.

224 COMMUNICATION IS A VITAL LINK Information gained from L.R. James, 1984. *System and Intervention, Adolescent Maltreatment: Issues and Program Models*, U.S. Department of Health and Human Services, Administration for Children, Youth and Families, Children's Bureau, National Center on Child Abuse

and Neglect, DHHS Publication No. (OHDS) 84-30339, Washington, D.C., Government Printing Office.

229 HELP IN CREATING THESE Suggestions obtained from *Planning and Implementing Child Abuse and Neglect Service Program: The Experiences of Eleven Demonstration Projects,* 1977, p. 91. This study was published by the National Center on Child Development/Office of Human Development, U.S. Department of Health, Education and Welfare, OHEW Publication No. (OHD) 77-300993, Washington, D.C.: Government Printing Office.

Additional References

Although many of the sources used in this book have been specifically referenced, the following were used in background information, conceptualizing theories or ideas, presenting a larger picture or otherwise informing the authors.

Ackerman, Robert J. *Growing in the Shadow: Children of Alcoholics*, 1986; *Same House Different Home: Why Adult Children of Alcoholics Are Not All The Same,* 1987; *Let Go And Grow: Recovery for Adult Children*, 1987; *Perfect Daughters: Adult Daughters of Alcoholics*, 1989, Deerfield Beach, Florida: Health Communications.

Anthony, James E. and Cohler, Bertram J. *The Invulnerable Child*, 1987, New York: The Guilford Press.

Additional References

Beattie, Melodie. *Codependent No More: How to Stop Controlling Others and Start Caring for Yourself*, 1987, New York, NY: Harper & Row.

Blueprint for Progress: Al-Anon's Fourth Step Inventory, 1976, New York: Al-Anon Family Group Headquarters Inc.

Broadhurst, D.D. & MacDicken, R.A., 1979. *Training in the prevention and treatment of child abuse and neglect*, National Center on Child Abuse and Neglect, Children's Bureau, Administration for Children, Youth and Families, Office of Human Development Services, U.S. Department of Health, Education and Welfare, DHEW Publication No. (OHDS) 79-30201.

Burgess, R.G. & Conger, R.D., 1978. Family interactions in abusive, neglectful and normal families. Child Development, 49, 1163- 1173.

Campagna, Daniel S. and Poffenberger, Donald L. *The Sexual Trafficking in Children: An Investigation of the Child Sex Trade*, 1988, Dover, Massachusetts: Auburn House Publishing Company.

Coombs, Robert H. *The Family Context of Adolescent Drug Use*, 1988, New York: The Haworth Press.

Florida Juvenile Handbook, 1986, Tallahassee, Florida: Florida Department of Law Enforcement.

Foreman, S. & Seligman, L., 1983, Adolescent abuse. *School Counselor*, 31(1), 17-25.

Keys, Ken Jr. *A Conscious Person's Guide to Relationships*, 1979, Marina del Rey, California: Living Love Publications.

MacPike, Loralee, (ed), *There's Something I've Been Meaning to Tell You*, 1989, Tallahassee, Florida: Naiad Press.

Mayhall, P. & Norgard, K., 1980. Foster parenting the abused and neglected child. Prinia College Advanced Foster Care Project, Tucson, Arizona. In Mayhall, P.D., & Norgard, K.E., 1983. *Child abuse and neglect*. New York: John Wiley & Sons.

Pianta, B., 1984. *Antecedents of child abuse: Single and multiple factor models*. New York: Columbia University Press.

Schwebel, Andrew, Schwebel, Bernice, Schwebel, Carol, Schwebel, Milton, Schwebel, Robert, *A Guide to a Happier Family: Overcoming the Anger, Frustration and Boredom that Destroy Family Life*, 1989, Los Angeles, California: Jeremy P. Tarcher Inc.

Soeffing, M., 1975. Abused children are exceptional children. *Exceptional Children*, 42, 129. In Garbarino, J. & Gilliam, G., 1980. *Understanding abusive families*. Massachusetts: Lexington Books.